UNCLE REMUS R

3 6353 0119850 0

P9-CAE-087

NEW SWAN SHAKESPEARE

GENERAL EDITOR
BERNARD LOTT, M.A.

*

Julius Caesar

DATE DUE	
2 1997	
8 1999	
WITHDRAWN	

PRINTED IN U.S.A.

WILLIAM SHAKESPEARE

Julius Caesar

EDITED BY

H. M. HULME, M.A., PH.D.

UNCLE REMUS
REGIONAL LIBRARY
1131 East Avenue
Madison, Georgia 30650

LONGMAN

0120498

Longman Group Limited
Longman House, Burnt Mill, Harlow
Essex CM20 2JE, England
Associated Companies throughout the world

© Longman Group Limited

All rights reserved; no part of this publication
may be reproduced, stored in a retrieval system
or transmitted in any form or by any means, electronic,
mechanical, photocopying, recording or otherwise,
without the prior written permission of the Publishers.

First published 1959
Reprinted 1986 (twice)

ISBN 0-582-52713-9

Illustrations by Clyde Pearson
Cover illustration by Caroline Holmes-Smith

We are indebted to the Local Examinations Syndicate,
Cambridge University, for permission to reproduce extracts
from the English Literature papers of the Cambridge School
Certificate (Overseas) and to the University of London for
extracts from the English Literature papers, General
Certificate of Education Ordinary Level.

Produced by Longman Group (FE) Ltd
Printed in Hong Kong

INTRODUCTION

The purpose of this book is to present one of Shakespeare's plays in the simplest and most direct way. The text itself, which forms the greater part of the book, is complete. Spelling and punctuation have been modernised; notes and a section giving hints to examination candidates have been added.

All explanations have been given within the range of a specially chosen list of 3,000 most commonly used English root-words. Words which are not used in Modern English as Shakespeare used them, or which are not now used at all, will be found explained in notes on the pages facing the text. Words in the play itself which are outside the 3,000-word vocabulary but which are still used with the same meaning in modern English are not necessarily explained in the notes. For such words you may need to use a dictionary such as the *Longman Dictionary of Contemporary English*, which explains them using a limited vocabulary of 2,000 words.

1 *The story of* Julius Caesar

In February, 44 B.C., Julius Caesar, a Roman statesman and general, returns to Rome after a great victory. The common people take a day's holiday to welcome him but the tribunes are afraid of Caesar's power and ambition. A man who claims that he can foretell the future warns Caesar that March 15th (called in the Roman calendar the Ides of March) will be a day of danger for him. Cassius and Brutus, with other Roman nobles, fear that Caesar wants to become king; they wish Italy to remain a republic. At a great ceremony Caesar is three times offered the crown by his friend and supporter, Mark Antony. He refuses it, although unwillingly. Brutus decides that Caesar must die and that he will join in the conspiracy against him. It is agreed that Caesar shall be killed on the Ides of March; Antony's life is to be spared.

But on this day, March 15th, Caesar's wife, frightened by the terrible storm of the previous night and by the hideous dream she has had, tries to make Caesar stay safely at home. Decius Brutus, however, another of the conspirators, flatters and shames

Caesar into going to the Capitol. There the conspirators ask that a man whom Caesar has banished from Rome may be allowed to return. When Caesar refuses, Casca and the rest stab him. Antony, allowed by Brutus to speak at Caesar's funeral, arouses the people against the conspirators; Cassius and Brutus have to flee for their lives.

Three men, Antony, Octavius (nephew of Julius Caesar) and Lepidus, become the rulers of Rome; they make a list of their enemies who are to die. Antony explains to Octavius that they will allow Lepidus to share their power only as long as it suits them to do so. Brutus and Cassius join forces near Sardis; Brutus has already heard that his wife Portia has killed herself in Rome. He and Cassius quarrel but become good friends again, and Cassius agrees, although unwillingly, that they shall march to Philippi to fight there against Antony and Octavius. The ghost of Caesar appears to Brutus; they are to meet again at Philippi. In the battle there, Antony and Octavius are victorious; Cassius, fearing capture and disgrace, asks his slave to kill him. Brutus runs on his own sword. So the spirit of Caesar is avenged.

2 The Play as Drama

As far as we know the play was first printed in 1623, seven years after Shakespeare's death. It was written, we think, in 1598–9. Latin was then the chief subject taught in schools, and people were very interested in the ancient history of Rome. Dramatists of Shakespeare's time would often base their plays on well-known stories or on actual history, and Shakespeare based his *Julius Caesar* on the stories of Caesar, Brutus and Antony in a collection of Lives of famous Greeks and Romans (written by Plutarch in the first century A.D.) which he had read in an English translation. On this foundation of slow-moving history he constructed his own exciting play, adding to and rearranging the things that actually happened, imagining the thoughts and feelings of his characters and writing all their speeches.

The theatre in Shakespeare's time was different in some ways from the theatre of today. For example, the stage stretched far out into the open space where the audience sat or stood – so far, in fact, that people were gathered round three sides of it. The fourth side extended back a considerable way, and formed a recess which was roofed over by a second floor. A good deal of action could be set on the upper floor itself; Antony might speak to the crowd from there (III.ii), until he asks "Shall I descend ?" and comes down to where the body of Caesar lies.

This old type of stage was most suitable, too, on the occasions when an actor speaks to himself, so as to let the audience know what he is thinking. Such passages often occur in Shakespeare's plays; and in his time the actor who was to speak them could walk to the front of the stage, in close contact with the audience. When Brutus is alone in his orchard, asking himself if Caesar must die for his ambition, he could so express his thoughts that those watching him seemed to be overhearing the words of a man who had come amongst them; they could share in his problem. So too when Caesar's ghost appears to him, the audience could feel the horror which Brutus felt and could also admire his courage.

In the public theatres plays were given in the afternoon, by daylight; as far as is known there was no special stage lighting and practically no scenery. This, as it happens, was to our advantage. For in place of painted scenery, Shakespeare put into the mouths of his characters splendid descriptions, poetry which paints the scenes in the mind's eye. On the night before Caesar's death we sense the terror of the great storm. As the night passes the characters themselves speak of "the progress of the stars", the break of dawn and the "raw cold morning".

Things happen more quickly within the play than they could in real life. Between the feast of the Lupercal (February 15th) when Caesar is offered the crown by Mark Antony, and the Ides of March (March 15th) when he is murdered, the interval of which the characters speak is not four weeks, but one night only, the night of the great storm.

3 *The Language of the Play*

Shakespeare's language differs in a number of ways from the English we speak today. In this section are listed a number of words, and parts of words, not used today as Shakespeare used them, which occur so often that it would be a waste of space to explain them each time they appeared in the text. These words have either a different meaning from that which we now give them, or are not used in everyday Modern English or are often shortened in Shakespeare's writing to fit in with the metrical pattern of the lines.

an – "if".

aught – "anything".

ay – "yes".

do, does, did are often used with another verb and without adding any separate meaning, e.g.

> And when the fit was on him I did mark
> How he did shake
> (I.ii.121)

e'er – "ever".

ere – "before".

hence – "from this place".

hereafter – "after this".

hither – "to this place".

methinks – "it seems to me".

mine – (sometimes) "my".

ne'er – "never".

nor – (sometimes) "neither".

or – (sometimes) "either".

presently – "at once".

prithee – "please" (short for "I pray thee").

quoth – "said".

sooth – "truth".

still – (sometimes) "always".

't – "it"; e.g. *on 't* – "on it".

thee – "you" (singular).

thence – "from that place".

thereafter – "after that".

thither – "to that place".

thou – "you" (singular).

This is the word often used as the second person singular subject; the verb associated with it ends in *-est* or *-st*, e.g.

What dost thou with thy best apparel on? (I.i.8). The verb *to be* and a few others are, however, irregular in this respect, e.g.

Thou art a cobbler, art thou? (I.i.23)

Take thou what course thou wilt. (III.ii.266)

whe'er – "whether".

whence – "from which place".

wherefore – "for what reason" (compare *therefore* – "for this reason").

whither – "to which place".

ye – "you" (plural).

yet – (sometimes) "again".

yon, yond – "that"

"of" is sometimes shortened to *o'*.

Most of the speeches are in what is called blank verse, i.e. the rhythm depends upon five stressed syllables in each line, the lines being without rhyme:

Withín my tént his bónes tonight shall líe (v.v.78).

This kind of verse is very suitable for a play as the pattern can be changed slightly from line to line to fit in with the natural rhythms of speech; the positions of the stressed syllables may vary and the stress may fall lightly on an unaccented syllable:

Thís was the nóblest Róman óf them áll

Áll the conspírators sáve ónly hé

Díd that they díd in énvy óf great Cáesar (v.v.68).

Sometimes at the end of a scene the lines rhyme in a couplet (two lines together)

And after this let Caesar seat him sure

For we will shake him or worse days endure (I.ii.314),

but more often, because of the speed of this play, the scenes end in a half-line, carrying us on quickly to the next part of the story (e.g. Act IV, Scene i; Act III, Scene i; Act v, Scene iv). The effect of the blank verse is to make the lines more easily remembered, as for instance,

Yond Cassius hath a lean and hungry look,

more noble,

Cowards die many times before their deaths,

more full of feeling,

I, that denied thee gold, will give my heart.

Prose is used by the humbler and more comic characters. In the first scene the tribunes, who are serious and responsible officers, speak mainly in verse, the carpenter and the cobbler in prose. Casca's bitter description of how Caesar is offered the crown is given in prose but at other times he speaks in verse. After the death of Caesar, Brutus speaks to the people in prose; when Cinna, the poet, is attacked by the crowd the speeches are in prose.

An important part of the language of poetry is imagery, which brings an idea (not actually true) of some picture ('image') or perhaps of a sound, a movement, a touch or even a scent, to add to the argument or feeling that is being spoken of. So, for example, Metellus thinks that they should ask Cicero to join in their plot against Caesar:

> his silver hairs
> Will purchase us a good opinion,
> And buy men's voices to commend our deeds
> (II.i.144).

We know that *hairs* cannot actually *buy voices*, but *silver* makes us see the shining hairs of the old Cicero as if they were shining silver coins and we understand very quickly the value to the conspirators of this wise old man; if he joins them, men will think their action wise and worthy of praise.

In *Julius Caesar* Shakespeare often uses *similes*; these are comparisons based on imagery and introduced by such words as *as* or *like*. Cassius says of Caesar

> he doth bestride the narrow world
> Like a Colossus (I.ii.135);

Brutus says of the threats of Cassius

> they pass by me as the idle wind
> Which I respect not (IV.iii.68).

Imagery takes the form of *metaphor* when a comparison is not mentioned as such, but suggested, as when Antony tells the crowd

> let me not stir you up
> To such a sudden *flood* of mutiny (III.ii.204)

and

> I come not, friends, to *steal* away your hearts
> (III.ii.210).

The kind of image in which a thing or idea is spoken of as a person is known as *personification*; Brutus thinks of *young ambition* climbing the ladder of lowliness (II.i.22); Caesar speaks of

Danger and himself as twin lions (II.ii.47); Antony describes how pity shall be choked when civil war comes upon Italy (III.i.278).

Shakespeare makes his words memorable in other ways than by imagery; for example, a character may surprise us by a very short speech as when Brutus tells Cassius

No man bears sorrow better. Portia is dead! (IV.iii.145).

Words which we heard much earlier in the play may be repeated in a different way. In the first scene one of the tribunes tells the people, when they are glad that Caesar has defeated Pompey's sons, that they are "blocks" and "stones". After the death of Caesar, Antony tells them, with equal truth,

You are not wood, you are not stones, but men (III.ii.140).

So too with the words *dumb mouths* (III.i.269 and III.ii.219) and with the word *pricked* (III.i.225 and IV.i.1).

Dramatic irony is used when a speech is written so as to be understood in one way by a certain character, while the audience, or another character, understands it to have some secret and special meaning. Because we know of the conspiracy, we see a secret meaning, which Caesar does not know about, in the speech of Decius interpreting Calpurnia's dream (II.ii. 84 ff). And if we are seeing or reading the play for a second time, there is an extra meaning for us in the words of Cinna, the poet,

I dreamt tonight that I did feast with Caesar (III.iii.1);

we know that Cinna will soon join Caesar in death. Other examples may be noted in Caesar's words about Cassius

He thinks too much; such men are dangerous (I.ii.195)

and in Portia's words to Lucius

Brutus hath a suit

That Caesar will not grant (II.iv.42);

a number of others will be found.

4 The Structure of the Play

There is no doubt that the play is very well constructed, but it is only when we look closely that we begin to notice how well: no words are wasted; everything we are told is for a purpose.

In the opening scene we laugh at the cobbler's jokes and we hear about Caesar's triumph. But we are shown also that it is easy to misunderstand the ordinary people of Rome: Marullus cannot at first understand the cobbler; Brutus will not know how to handle the crowd after the death of Caesar. It is easy also to change the mood of the people; Antony will know how to do this.

The second scene gives us much more information: Caesar has no son to take power after him; he is known to be in danger; he shows no affection for his wife; his wishes are obeyed. All this Shakespeare shows us in the first few lines. Next we learn of the friendship which Cassius has for Brutus. (This is in the end to destroy both men: Brutus dies because Cassius persuades him to join the conspiracy, Cassius because he gives way to Brutus as to where the battle is to be fought.) From Cassius we hear that Caesar is neither young nor strong; he is as powerful as a god and Cassius is jealous of him. Caesar's words show that he is aware of this jealousy. No time is wasted in giving us all the speeches that might be made when the crown is offered to Caesar; we hear through Casca of those details which are important. The scene ends with Cassius planning to win over Brutus. Next comes an exciting description of the night's storm and Cassius talks to Casca as we can imagine he has talked to many others. Before daybreak Brutus is also to be persuaded. We realise how much has happened in the first act, the first day.

The second act begins with the struggle in the mind of Brutus. The plan for Caesar's murder is fairly quickly made, Brutus insisting that Antony's life is spared. Brutus is given most of the speeches in this scene; his love for Portia is shown so that we may sympathise with him even more. The next scenes keep us uncertain of what will happen: will Caesar go to the Senate House; will Artemidorus or the Soothsayer give the message that will save him? The anxiety of Portia makes the audience more anxious. It is now the morning of the second day.

In the third act we reach the centre, the climax, of the play. Things happen quickly in the first scene; any hope that Caesar will be warned in time is over within a few lines; the plan for his murder is put into effect. Then the action slows down again. Shakespeare must show us, for the first time, the strength of Antony's feelings; we know that he will take revenge. In the next scene, the middle scene of the play, Brutus first and then Antony speak to the people. Antony gains their support and Brutus and Cassius have to flee from the city. Then comes the short scene of cruel humour in which Cinna, the poet, is killed by the foolish crowd: Antony has done his work too well. This is the evening of the second day.

Now comes an interval of time; with the beginning of Act IV the play is moving to its end. We see at once the hard and calculating side of Antony's character; he is not so noble as Brutus; perhaps, therefore, he will be more successful. The second scene brings us back to Brutus and Cassius, their friendship and their difficulties. Brutus, who cannot get money by harsh and cruel means, asks Cassius to supply him. We hear of Portia's death, and are prepared for the approaching end of Brutus and Cassius. Caesar's ghost appears to Brutus, reminding us of the reason for the civil war.

Act V begins with the leaders of the two sides accusing each other: Brutus was a false friend to Caesar, Antony has been responsible for the deaths of many. Cassius, we see, is afraid of the omens. On the battle-field a number of separate happenings are very quickly shown; we understand the difficulty of sending messages and getting news. Brutus advances too soon; Cassius is too quick to think himself defeated. For some time we see only the generals and soldiers of the losing side. Brutus tells how he has seen again the ghost of Caesar. The play ends with his death and the words of Antony and Octavius in his praise.

5 The Characters of the Play

We are able to believe in Shakespeare's characters because he makes them neither wholly good nor wholly bad, and we learn bit by bit what kind of people they are.

Caesar's power is feared by the tribunes but Artemidorus admires Caesar as a just man and the Soothsayer tries to save his life. Although Cassius hates Caesar, Brutus likes him; he would not wish him to be king in Rome, yet he knows 'no personal cause' to attack him. We are told something of Caesar's physical weakness by Cassius and by Casca; Decius knows how easily he can be flattered. Yet Antony looks on Caesar as the noblest of men; he has been a brave general and a generous ruler. Caesar's own words show him as very proud, but we cannot deny his courage.

Brutus is more sympathetically presented; he loves his wife and is very kind to his young servant; all men speak of him as noble and honourable. Caesar admires him; Antony and Octavius, his enemies, respect him. Perhaps, however, he is too noble: he lets Cassius persuade him to join the conspiracy but he will not agree that Antony shall also be killed. He cannot take money from poor farmers, but instead he asks Cassius to give him money to pay his soldiers. At the same time he accuses Cassius of being greedy for money. When Cassius loses confidence just before Caesar is murdered, Brutus remains strong in purpose; on the other hand he makes the mistake of attacking too early in their battle.

Cassius seems to us a real person because his faults are so human. He is proud and quick to anger. Although at first he seems to have a stronger character than Brutus, he gives way to him later in important decisions.

Shakespeare makes *Antony* a real person by showing us first one side of his character and then another. At first he is a young man who enjoys the pleasures of life, and we think, with Trebonius, that there is no need to fear him. But he loves Caesar deeply and makes a great effort to win the crowd to his side. He does not, like Brutus, think first of what is best for Rome. When next we see him, he is a calculating ruler, listing the names of men who are to die. But, having won the battle, he is kind and generous to the soldiers and servants of the dead Brutus.

DRAMATIS PERSONAE

JULIUS CAESAR
OCTAVIUS CAESAR   } *Triumvirs after the death of Julius*
MARCUS ANTONIUS   *Caesar*
M. AEMILIUS LEPIDUS

CICERO
PUBLIUS   } *Senators*
POPILIUS LENA

MARCUS BRUTUS
CASSIUS
CASCA
TREBONIUS
LIGARIUS   } *conspirators against Julius Caesar*
DECIUS BRUTUS
METELLUS CIMBER
CINNA

FLAVIUS AND MARULLUS, *Tribunes*
ARTEMIDORUS
A SOOTHSAYER
CINNA, a poet
ANOTHER POET

LUCILIUS
TITINIUS
MESSALA   } *friends of Brutus and Cassius*
YOUNG CATO
VOLUMNIUS

VARRO
CLITUS
CLAUDIUS
STRATO   } *servants of Brutus*
LUCIUS
DARDANIUS

PINDARUS, *servant of Cassius*
CALPURNIA, *wife of Caesar*
PORTIA, *wife of Brutus*

SENATORS, CITIZENS, GUARDS

The scenes are laid in Rome; the neighbourhood of Sardis (IV.ii and IV.iii); the neighbourhood of Philippi (V).

1 The day is February 15th, 44 B.C. Flavius and Marullus, two officials whose duty it is to defend the rights of the common people against the nobles, are angry that the working people have taken a holiday to welcome Caesar home after his victory over Pompey's two sons. Marullus reminds the people how much they used to admire Pompey (a great Roman, Caesar's rival, now dead). Ashamed and silent the people go to their homes. The tribunes, afraid of Caesar's ambition and power, take down from the statues the decorations which have been put up in Caesar's honour. In this scene we see how quickly the mood of the people may be changed.

2 *Being mechanical . . . your profession* – "since you belong to the working (*mechanical*) classes, you ought not to go out on a working (*labouring*) day without having something with you to show the kind of work you do".

3 *what trade art thou?* – "what is your job?"

4 *Truly, sir, . . . cobbler* – "To tell you the truth (*truly*), sir, in comparison with (*in respect of*) a man doing delicate (*fine*) work, I am only (*but*) what you would call an unskilful patcher". The word *cobbler* had two meanings, 'shoe-mender' and 'unskilful patcher'; Shakespeare's cobbler here is making a pun, i.e. playing on both senses.

5 *directly* – "at once"; also "with a straight, clear answer".

6 *use* – "work at".

7 *soles*. The cobbler is making a second pun; he mends *soles*, but lets Marullus think he mends *souls*.

8 *knave* – "wicked fellow".

9 *naughty* – "disobedient, disrespectful".

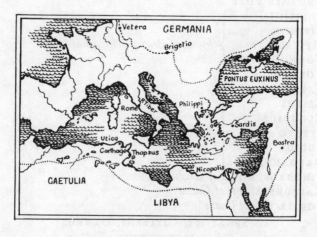

Map showing places named in the play

JULIUS CAESAR

ACT ONE

Scene I. A street in Rome.[1]
Enter FLAVIUS, MARULLUS *and certain* Commoners.

FLAVIUS

Hence! Home, you idle creatures, get you home!
Is this a holiday? What, know you not
Being mechanical, you ought not walk
Upon a labouring day without the sign
Of your profession?[2] Speak, what trade art thou?[3]   5

CARPENTER

Why, sir, a carpenter.

MARULLUS

Where is thy leather apron and thy rule?
What dost thou with thy best apparel on?
You, sir, what trade are you?

COBBLER

Truly, sir, in respect of a fine workman, I am but, as you would   10
say, a cobbler.[4]

MARULLUS

But what trade art thou? Answer me directly.[5]

COBBLER

A trade, sir, that I hope I may use[6] with a safe conscience,
which is indeed, sir, a mender of bad soles.[7]

FLAVIUS

What trade, thou knave?[8] Thou naughty[9] knave, what trade?   15

1

10 *be not out ... out* – "don't be out of *temper* with me; but if your feet are coming *out of your shoes ...*" (another pun).

11 *live by* – "earn my living with".

12 *recover them* – "save their lives"; also "put patches on (*re-cover*)".

13 *proper* – "good, true".

14 *neat's* – "ox's".

15 *gone* – "walked".

16 *to get myself into* – "to find myself".

17 *in his triumph* – "because of his victory procession". The two sons of Pompey had wished to take revenge on Caesar for their father's defeat by him. In a great battle against them, at Munda, in Spain, Caesar was once more victorious and returned to Rome where he was granted the right of a triumphal procession.

18 *conquest* – "prizes of victory". Caesar's victory was over Romans only; no new territory had been won.

19 *tributaries* – "kings or princes who have become our subjects".

20 *To grace ... his chariot wheels* – "to do him honour as they walk by his chariot in prisoners' chains".

21 *blocks* – "stupid, unfeeling lumps".

22 *senseless* – "without feeling".

all that I live by is with the awl

2

COBBLER

Nay, I beseech you, sir, be not out with me; yet if you be out,[10]
sir, I can mend you.

MARULLUS

What meanest thou by that? Mend me, thou saucy fellow?

COBBLER

Why, sir, cobble you.

FLAVIUS

Thou art a cobbler, art thou?   20

COBBLER

Truly, sir, all that I live by[11] is with the awl. I meddle with no
tradesman's matters, nor women's matters, but with all. I am
indeed, sir, a surgeon to old shoes; when they are in great
danger, I recover them.[12] As proper[13] men as ever trod upon
neat's[14] leather have gone[15] upon my handiwork.   25

FLAVIUS

But wherefore art not in thy shop today?
Why dost thou lead these men about the streets?

COBBLER

Truly, sir, to wear out their shoes, to get myself into[16] more
work. But indeed, sir, we make holiday to see Caesar, and to
rejoice in his triumph.[17]   30

MARULLUS

Wherefore rejoice? What conquest[18] brings he home?
What tributaries[19] follow him to Rome
To grace in captive bonds his chariot wheels?[20]
You blocks,[21] you stones, you worse than senseless[22] things!
O you hard hearts, you cruel men of Rome,   35

23 *Pompey*. Pompey and Caesar had been rivals for power. Caesar defeated Pompey at the battle of Pharsalia and Pompey fled into Egypt where he was put to death.

24 *yea* – "yes, even".

25 *The live-long day* – "the whole day long".

26 *but appear* – "appear in the distance, only just in sight".

27 *made an universal shout* – "shouted all together".

28 *That Tiber trembled . . . concave shores* – "so that (*That*) even the river Tiber was stirred with fear as she heard the echo (*replication*) of your shouts in her curving (*concave*) banks".

29 *cull out* – "choose to have".

30 *in his way, That* – "in the path of one who . . ."

31 *blood* – "flesh and blood", i.e. Pompey's two sons.

32 *intermit* – "keep back".

33 *needs must light on* – "must certainly fall as a punishment upon . . ."

34 *for this fault* – "to show that you are sorry for what you have done wrong".

35 *sort* – "class".

36 *Draw them to Tiber banks . . . of all* – "lead them to the banks of the Tiber and let your tears fall into the river (*channel*) until the water rises from its lowest level to reach the highest point of the bank".

37 *See whe'er their basest metal . . . moved* – "See whether (*whe'er*) their most worthless quality, their mean and insincere character (base metals were non-precious) is not touched with feeling".

38 *Capitol*, a hill in Rome on which stood a great temple.

39 *Disrobe the images . . . ceremonies* – "Take the scarves and ribbons from the statues if you find them decorated with these signs of rejoicing".

40 *feast of Lupercal*, February 15th. Spring festival (when sacrifice was offered so that the earth might again be fruitful).

And when you saw his chariot but appear

Knew you not Pompey?[23] Many a time and oft
Have you climbed up to walls and battlements,
To towers and windows; yea,[24] to chimney tops,
Your infants in your arms, and there have sat
The live-long day,[25] with patient expectation,   40
To see great Pompey pass the streets of Rome;
And when you saw his chariot but appear,[26]
Have you not made an universal shout,[27]
That Tiber trembled underneath her banks
To hear the replication of your sounds   45
Made in her concave shores?[28]
And do you now put on your best attire?
And do you now cull out[29] a holiday?
And do you now strew flowers in his way
That[30] comes in triumph over Pompey's blood?[31]   50
Be gone!
Run to your houses, fall upon your knees,
Pray to the gods to intermit[32] the plague
That needs must light on[33] this ingratitude.

FLAVIUS

Go, go, good countrymen, and, for this fault,[34]   55
Assemble all the poor men of your sort;[35]
Draw them to Tiber banks, and weep your tears
Into the channel, till the lowest stream
Do kiss the most exalted shores of all.[36]

[*Exeunt all the* Commoners

See whe'er their basest metal be not moved;[37]   60
They vanish tongue-tied in their guiltiness.
Go you down that way towards the Capitol;[38]
This way will I. Disrobe the images,
If you do find them decked with ceremonies.[39]

MARULLUS

May we do so?   65
You know it is the feast of Lupercal.[40]

41 *It is no matter* – "That does not matter".

42 *Caesar's trophies* – "signs of Caesar's victory".

43 *I'll about* – "I will go through the town".

44 *vulgar* – "ordinary, common people".

45 *So do you too . . . thick* – "You do the same where you see them crowded together".

46 *These growing feathers . . . fearfulness* – "If we pull out these feathers from Caesar's wing before they have had time to grow, we shall keep him from flying too high (*pitch*, 'height'), for he is a man who otherwise would fly high (*soar*) out of sight, and keep us all in fear like slaves." They would never know when he would come suddenly down like an eagle or hawk to attack them.

1 Caesar's superstition is shown in his words to his wife and to Mark Antony, but when the soothsayer warns him that he will be in great danger on March 15th, he pays no attention. Cassius blames Brutus for being less friendly than before. Brutus answers that he is not unfriendly, but very worried. Hearing the applause of the crowd, Brutus is afraid that the people will make Caesar king of Rome. Cassius describes Caesar's weakness; once he had to save him from drowning and he looked after him in Spain when Caesar had a fever. Yet now, he goes on, Caesar is the greatest man in Rome and has become all-powerful. As the procession comes back, Caesar looks very angry. Casca describes to Brutus and Cassius how Mark Antony had three times offered Caesar a crown, but Caesar refused it, realising that the people did not want him to accept. This so angered Caesar that he fell down in a fit in the market-place. Casca tells them also that the two tribunes, Flavius and Marullus, have been put out of office for pulling the decorations from Caesar's statues. Cassius plans to throw letters, written in different handwritings, in at the windows of Brutus' house. The letters will speak of Caesar's ambition and will say how much the name of Brutus is valued in Rome.

2 *for the course* – "ready for the running". On the feast of the Lupercalia, young noblemen would run naked through the streets, carrying strips of leather with which they would pretend to strike all the people in their way. Women who wanted children would stand in their path and hold out their hands to be struck, since they believed that this would bring them what they wished.

3 *Peace, ho!* – "Silence, I say".

4 *directly in Antonius' way . . . his course* – "right in the path of Antony when he runs the way he is to go".

6

FLAVIUS

It is no matter.[41] Let no images
Be hung with Caesar's trophies.[42] I'll about,[43]
And drive away the vulgar[44] from the streets;
So do you too, where you perceive them thick.[45]   70
These growing feathers, plucked from Caesar's wing,
Will make him fly an ordinary pitch,
Who else would soar above the view of men,
And keep us all in servile fearfulness.[46]

[*Exeunt*

Scene II. *A public place.*[1]

Flourish. Enter CAESAR, ANTONY, *for the course,*[2]
CALPURNIA, PORTIA, DECIUS, CICERO, BRUTUS,
CASSIUS *and* CASCA; *a great crowd following, among them a*
Soothsayer.

CAESAR

Calpurnia!

CASCA

Peace, ho![3] Caesar speaks.

CAESAR

Calpurnia!

CALPURNIA

Here, my lord.

CAESAR

Stand you directly in Antonius' way,
When he doth run his course.[4] Antonius!

ANTONY

Caesar, my lord?   5

7

5 *in your speed* – "as you are running fast".

6 *elders* – "old people".

7 *Shake off their sterile curse* – "throw off the misfortune of childlessness".

8 *Set on* – "Begin".

9 *in the press . . . on me* – "in the crowd that calls my name".

10 *Beware the Ides of March!* – "Expect danger on March 15th". In the Roman calendar, dates were calculated from certain named days; the Ides fell on the thirteenth of certain months, on the fifteenth of others.

CAESAR

Forget not in your speed,[5] Antonius,
To touch Calpurnia, for our elders[6] say,
The barren touchéd in this holy chase,
Shake off their sterile curse.[7]

ANTONY

              I shall remember;
When Caesar says "Do this!" it is performed.   10

CAESAR

Set on,[8] and leave no ceremony out.

SOOTHSAYER

Caesar!

CAESAR

Ha? Who calls?

CASCA

Bid every noise be still! Peace yet again!

CAESAR

Who is it in the press that calls on me?[9]   15
I hear a tongue shriller than all the music
Cry, "Caesar." Speak! Caesar is turned to hear.

SOOTHSAYER

Beware the Ides of March![10]

CAESAR

           What man is that?

BRUTUS

A soothsayer bids you beware the Ides of March.

11 *Pass* – "Let us go".
12 *Sennet*. Trumpet sounds.
13 *the order of the course* – "the way the men run".
14 *gamesome* – "interested in sport".
15 *quick spirit* – "character so full of life"

10

CAESAR

Set him before me; let me see his face.   20

CASSIUS

Fellow, come from the throng; look upon Caesar.

CAESAR

What sayst thou to me now? Speak once again.

SOOTHSAYER

Beware the Ides of March!

CAESAR

He is a dreamer. Let us leave him. Pass.[11]

> [*Sennet.*[12] *Exeunt all but* BRUTUS *and* CASSIUS

CASSIUS

Will you go see the order of the course?[13]   25

BRUTUS

Not I.

CASSIUS

I pray you, do.

BRUTUS

I am not gamesome.[14] I do lack some part
Of that quick spirit[15] that is in Antony.
Let me not hinder, Cassius, your desires;   30
I 'll leave you.

11

16 *I do observe . . . wont to have* – "I have seen (*do observe*) for some time (*now of late*) that I no longer get from you the looks of kindness and friendship (*gentleness and show of love*) that I used (*was wont*) to have".

17 *You bear too stubborn . . . friend* – "You make yourself appear too hard (*stubborn*) and too unfriendly (*strange*) to me" (*bear a hand over*, 'put on an appearance to').

18 *If I have veiled . . . upon myself.* "If I have not been open and friendly with you (*have veiled my look*), the reason for my worried expression (*the trouble of my countenance*) is only (*merely*) that I am myself upset".

19 *Vexéd I am . . . behaviours* – "I have lately been troubled with different feelings (*passions*), ideas (*conceptions*) belonging (*proper*) only to me, which make my behaviour less pleasant".

20 (*Among which number, Cassius, be you one*) – "(And let me count you, Cassius, among my friends)".

21 *Nor construe any further . . . to other men* – "Nor understand anything else from my coolness (*neglect*) except that poor Brutus, fighting out his own problems, forgets to show his friendship to others".

22 *much mistook your passion* – "greatly mistaken your feeling".

23 *By means whereof . . . hath buried* – "so that as a result my own heart has kept hidden . . ."

24 *sees not itself . . . some other things* – "can only see itself mirrored in something else".

CASSIUS

Brutus, I do observe you now of late,
I have not from your eyes that gentleness
And show of love as I was wont to have.[16]
You bear too stubborn and too strange a hand   35
Over your friend[17] that loves you.

BRUTUS

                    Cassius,
Be not deceived. If I have veiled my look,
I turn the trouble of my countenance
Merely upon myself.[18] Vexéd I am
Of late with passions of some difference,   40
Conceptions only proper to myself,
Which give some soil, perhaps, to my behaviours;[19]
But let not therefore my good friends be grieved
(Among which number, Cassius, be you one),[20]
Nor construe any further my neglect,   45
Than that poor Brutus, with himself at war,
Forgets the shows of love to other men.[21]

CASSIUS

Then, Brutus, I have much mistook your passion,[22]
By means whereof this breast of mine hath buried[23]
Thoughts of great value, worthy cogitations.   50
Tell me, good Brutus, can you see your face?

BRUTUS

No, Cassius;
For the eye sees not itself but by reflection
By some other things.[24]

CASSIUS

'T is just,   55
And it is very much lamented, Brutus,

13

25 *'T is just . . . into your eye* – "That is true, and many people are sorry that you have no such mirrors which will show to your own eyes your hidden nobility".

26 *best respect* – "noblest reputation".

27 *groaning underneath this age's yoke* – "suffering under the oppression of this time".

28 *had his eyes* – "might see as the others see".

29 *Therefore* – "The reason for it . . ."

30 *Will modestly discover to yourself* – "will, without making it too important (*modestly*), show (*discover*) you . . ."

31 *jealous on me* – "suspicious of me".

32 *Were I a common laughter* – "if I were laughed at by everybody". [This line is sometimes given *Were I a common laugher*, meaning "If I were one who laughs at everything."]

33 *or did use To stale . . . protester* – "or if I were always taking the freshness off my affection (*did use To stale my love*) by making vows every day (*with ordinary oaths*) to every new friend who promised loyalty (*to every new protester*)".

34 *after scandal them* – "afterwards speak evil of them".

35 *profess myself in banqueting . . . dangerous* – "tell all my affairs (*profess myself*), while feasting (*banqueting*), to all the crowd (*rout*), in that case (*then*) believe me to be (*hold me*) a dangerous friend".

14

That you have no mirrors as will turn
Your hidden worthiness into your eye,[25]
That you might see your shadow. I have heard,
Where many of the best respect[26] in Rome   60
(Except immortal Caesar), speaking of Brutus,
And groaning underneath this age's yoke,[27]
Have wished that noble Brutus had his eyes.[28]

BRUTUS

Into what dangers would you lead me, Cassius,
That you would have me seek into myself   65
For that which is not in me?

CASSIUS

Therefore,[29] good Brutus, be prepared to hear.
And, since you know you cannot see yourself
So well as by reflection, I, your glass,
Will modestly discover to yourself[30]   70
That of yourself which you yet know not of.
And be not jealous on me,[31] gentle Brutus.
Were I a common laughter,[32] or did use
To stale with ordinary oaths my love
To every new protester,[33] if you know,   75
That I do fawn on men, and hug them hard,
And after scandal them,[34] or if you know,
That I profess myself in banqueting
To all the rout, then hold me dangerous.[35]

[*Flourish, and shout*

BRUTUS

What means this shouting? I do fear the people   80
Choose Caesar for their king.

CASSIUS

          Ay, do you fear it?
Then must I think you would not have it so.

15

36 *If it be aught ... in th' other* – "If it is anything (*aught*) which is for the good of Rome (*toward the general good*), let me see honour and death side by side ..."

37 *indifferently* – "with equal calm".

38 *so speed me* – "so grant me success".

39 *as* – "in so far as ..."

40 *virtue* – "nobility".

41 *favour* – "appearance".

42 *for my single self ... thing* – "for myself alone, I would just as soon (*had as lief*) not exist, as go on living and be afraid of (*In awe of*) such a small creature ..."

43 *The troubled Tiber ... shores* – "when the stormy river Tiber was beating against her banks".

44 *flood* – "water".

45 *Upon the word* – "Even as he was speaking".

46 *Accoutred* – "dressed".

47 *we did buffet it ... controversy* – "we struck against it (*did buffet it*) with strong muscles (*lusty sinews*), tossing our way through it (*throwing it aside*) and defying (*stemming*) it with the courage (*hearts*) of opposition (*controversy*)".

48 *arrive the point proposed* – "get to the point we had agreed upon ..."

49 *as Aeneas ... bear.* Aeneas, a Trojan prince, hero of Roman story, carried his old father Anchises from the burning city of Troy, when the Greeks, after a ten years' struggle, captured the town and set it on fire. Aeneas came to Italy and settled there. After his death he was worshipped as a god.

BRUTUS

I would not, Cassius, yet I love him well.
But wherefore do you hold me here so long?
What is it that you would impart to me?   85
If it be aught toward the general good,
Set honour in one eye, and death in th' other,[36]
And I will look on both indifferently;[37]
For let the gods so speed me[38] as[39] I love
The name of honour more than I fear death.   90

CASSIUS

I know that virtue[40] to be in you, Brutus,
As well as I do know your outward favour.[41]
Well, honour is the subject of my story.
I cannot tell what you and other men
Think of this life, but, for my single self,   95
I had as lief not be, as live to be
In awe of such a thing[42] as I myself.
I was born free as Caesar; so were you;
We both have fed as well, and we can both
Endure the winter's cold as well as he.   100
For once, upon a raw and gusty day,
The troubled Tiber chafing with her shores,[43]
Caesar said to me "Dar'st thou, Cassius, now
Leap in with me into this angry flood,[44]
And swim to yonder point?" Upon the word,[45]   105
Accoutred[46] as I was, I plungéd in,
And bade him follow; so indeed he did.
The torrent roared, and we did buffet it
With lusty sinews, throwing it aside,
And stemming it with hearts of controversy.[47]   110
But ere we could arrive the point proposed,[48]
Caesar cried "Help me, Cassius, or I sink!"
Ay, as Aeneas, our great ancestor,
Did from the flames of Troy, upon his shoulder
The old Anchises bear,[49] so from the waves of Tiber   115

17

50 *become a god* – "looked upon, even during his lifetime, as a god".

51 *fit* – "height of the fever" (The fever came and went).

52 *His coward . . . fly* – "his lips turned pale. The blood seemed to fly from them as cowards fly from their flag (*colour*) in battle".

53 *whose bend doth awe . . . his lustre* – "whose glance (*bend*) terrifies the world lost its (*his*) healthy brightness".

54 *As* – "like".

55 *A man of such . . . alone* – "a man so feebly made should win so high a place in this splendid world and gain the prize (*bear the palm*) alone". (Metals are 'tempered' to make them strong; *get the start of*, 'get ahead in the race against'.)

56 *general shout* – "shout from the whole crowd".

57 *Colossus*, a great bronze statue; probably here the great statue of the god Apollo which stood astride one of the entrances to the harbour of Rhodes (a Greek city). This statue was one of the seven wonders of the ancient world.

58 *Men at some time . . . underlings* – "At some time of their lives men have the power to control what they will become. If we are under the control of others (*underlings*) we must blame, not the stars under which we were born (*our stars*), but our own characters".

59 *What should be in that "Caesar"?* – "What magic is there supposed to be in that name 'Caesar'?"

60 *be sounded more* – "be spoken more often . . ."

61 *fair* – "good".

62 *Sound them . . . as well* – "say them and 'Brutus' is as pleasant to say".

Like a Colossus[57]

18

Did I the tired Caesar: and this man
Is now become a god,[50] and Cassius is
A wretched creature, and must bend his body
If Caesar carelessly but nod on him.
He had a fever when he was in Spain,   120
And, when the fit[51] was on him, I did mark
How he did shake; 't is true, this god did shake;
His coward lips did from their colour fly,[52]
And that same eye, whose bend doth awe the world,
Did lose his lustre;[53] I did hear him groan.   125
Ay, and that tongue of his, that bade the Romans
Mark him, and write his speeches in their books,
"Alas," it cried, "give me some drink, Titinius,"
As[54] a sick girl. Ye gods, it doth amaze me,
A man of such a feeble temper should   130
So get the start of the majestic world,
And bear the palm alone.[55]

[*Shout. Flourish*

BRUTUS
                    Another general shout?[56]
I do believe that these applauses are
For some new honours that are heaped on Caesar.

CASSIUS
Why, man, he doth bestride the narrow world   135
Like a Colossus,[57] and we petty men
Walk under his huge legs, and peep about
To find ourselves dishonourable graves.
Men at some time are masters of their fates.
The fault, dear Brutus, is not in our stars,   140
But in ourselves, that we are underlings.[58]
"Brutus" and "Caesar": What should be in that "Caesar"?[59]
Why should that name be sounded more[60] than yours?
Write them together, yours is as fair[61] a name;
Sound them, it doth become the mouth as well.[62]   145

19

63 *Conjure* – "Work magic in calling up spirits".

64 *start* – "suddenly bring forth".

65 *meat* – "food".

66 *Age, thou art shamed* – "How much the people of this present day deserve to feel ashamed!"

67 *the breed of noble bloods* – "the power to produce noble sons".

68 *went there by an age . . . but it was famed* – "did there pass a period of history . . . which was not made famous . . ."

69 *encompassed but one man* – "contained one man only".

70 *Rome indeed, and room enough.* *Rome* and *room* ('space'), had the same pronunciation in Shakespeare's day. Cassius means that Rome is still called by its great name, but it has lost its greatness and has space now only for Caesar.

71 *but one only man* – "no one else except one man only".

72 *brooked The eternal devil . . . king* – "allowed (*brooked*) the everlasting devil to live splendidly (*keep his state*) in Rome as willingly (*easily*) as they would have accepted a king there". It was this ancestor of Brutus who drove out Tarquin, the last of the kings of Rome.

73 *That you do . . . jealous* – "That you are my friend I know; I am not suspicious (*jealous*) of you".

74 *work* – "persuade".

75 *aim* – "idea".

76 *For this present . . . moved* – "For the present, if I might ask you this in friendship, I would like you not to try to persuade me any more".

77 *find a time Both meet* – "find an opportunity suitable both . . ."

78 *high* – "important".

79 *chew upon this* – "keep this in your thoughts . . ."

80 *to repute himself . . . upon us* – "to count (*repute*) himself a Roman on conditions so difficult to accept as this present time is likely to force upon us".

81 *but thus much show of fire* – "even this amount of feeling".

Weigh them, it is as heavy. Conjure[63] with them,
"Brutus" will start[64] a spirit as soon as "Caesar".
Now in the names of all the gods at once,
Upon what meat[65] doth this our Caesar feed
That he is grown so great? Age, thou art shamed![66]   150
Rome, thou hast lost the breed of noble bloods![67]
When went there by an age, since the great flood,
But it was famed[68] with more than with one man?
When could they say, till now, that talked of Rome,
That her wide walls encompassed but one man?[69]   155
Now is it Rome indeed, and room enough,[70]
When there is in it but one only man.[71]
O, you and I have heard our fathers say
There was a Brutus once, that would have brooked
The eternal devil to keep his state in Rome,   160
As easily as a king.[72]

BRUTUS

That you do love me I am nothing jealous;[73]
What you would work[74] me to, I have some aim.[75]
How I have thought of this, and of these times,
I shall recount hereafter. For this present,   165
I would not, so with love I might entreat you,
Be any further moved.[76] What you have said
I will consider; what you have to say
I will with patience hear, and find a time
Both meet[77] to hear, and answer, such high[78] things.   170
Till then, my noble friend, chew upon this:[79]
Brutus had rather be a villager,
Than to repute himself a son of Rome
Under these hard conditions as this time
Is like to lay upon us.[80]   175

CASSIUS

I am glad that my weak words
Have struck but thus much show of fire[81] from Brutus.

21

82 *after his sour fashion* – "in his usual bitter way of speaking".

83 *What hath proceeded worthy note* – "what has happened worth remembering . . ."

84 *his train* – "the procession of people following him".

85 *The angry spot . . . brow* – "Caesar's face is red with anger" (*brow*, 'forehead').

86 *Being crossed . . . Senators* – "when some of the Councillors have disagreed (*crossed*) with him in discussion (*conference*)".

87 *what the matter is* – "what has gone wrong". (*Matter* meant something rather more important then than now.)

88 *o' nights* – "at night".

BRUTUS

The games are done and Caesar is returning.

CASSIUS

As they pass by, pluck Casca by the sleeve,
And he will, after his sour fashion,[82] tell you   180
What hath proceeded worthy note[83] today.

Re-enter CAESAR *and his train*[84]

BRUTUS

I will do so. But, look you, Cassius,
The angry spot doth glow on Caesar's brow,[85]
And all the rest look like a chidden train;
Calpurnia's cheek is pale, and Cicero   185
Looks with such ferret and such fiery eyes
As we have seen him in the Capitol,
Being crossed in conference by some Senators.[86]

CASSIUS

Casca will tell us what the matter is.[87]

CAESAR

Antonius!   190

ANTONY

Caesar.

CAESAR

Let me have men about me that are fat,
Sleek-headed men, and such as sleep o' nights.[88]
Yond Cassius has a lean and hungry look.
He thinks too much; such men are dangerous.   195

23

89 *well given* – "of honourable character".
90 *Would* – "I wish that ..."
91 *if my name were liable to fear* – "if the name of Caesar were subject to fear".

92 *sort* – "way".
93 *at heart's ease ... than themselves* – "contented in their hearts as long as they can see a man who is more powerful than they are".
94 *chanced* – "happened".

ANTONY

Fear him not, Caesar; he 's not dangerous;
He is a noble Roman, and well given. [89]

CAESAR

Would[90] he were fatter! But I fear him not.
Yet if my name were liable to fear,[91]
I do not know the man I should avoid   200
So soon as that spare Cassius. He reads much,
He is a great observer, and he looks
Quite through the deeds of men. He loves no plays,
As thou dost, Antony; he hears no music;
Seldom he smiles, and smiles in such a sort[92]   205
As if he mocked himself, and scorned his spirit
That could be moved to smile at anything.
Such men as he be never at heart's ease
Whiles they behold a greater than themselves,[93]
And therefore are they very dangerous.   210
I rather tell thee what is to be feared
Than what I fear, for always I am Caesar.
Come on my right hand, for this ear is deaf,
And tell me truly what thou thinkst of him.

[*Sennet. Exeunt* CAESAR *and his train, all but* CASCA

CASCA

You pulled me by the cloak; would you speak with me?   215

BRUTUS

Ay, Casca; tell us what hath chanced[94] today
That Caesar looks so sad.

CASCA

Why, you were with him, were you not?

25

95 *being offered him, he put it by* –
"when it was offered to him, he
pushed it aside (*put it by*) . . ."
96 *fell a-shouting* – "began to shout".
97 *Ay, merry, was 't* – "Yes, indeed it
was".

98 *gentler than other* – "less firmly than
the time before".
99 *at every putting-by* – "every time
he put it aside . . ."

BRUTUS

I should not then ask Casca what had chanced.

CASCA

Why, there was a crown offered him; and being offered him, 220
he put it by[95] with the back of his hand thus, and then the
people fell a-shouting.[96]

BRUTUS

What was the second noise for?

CASCA

Why, for that too.

CASSIUS

They shouted thrice. What was the last cry for? 225

CASCA

Why, for that too.

BRUTUS

Was the crown offered him thrice?

CASCA

Ay, marry, was 't,[97] and he put it by thrice, every time gentler
than other;[98] and at every putting-by[99] mine honest neighbours
shouted. 230

CASSIUS

Who offered him the crown?

CASCA

Why, Antony.

100 *Tell us . . . gentle Casca* – "Tell us how it was, my dear Casca".

101 *I can as well be hanged as tell* – "If I were to be hanged for not describing it, I still would not know how to tell you . . ."

102 *fain* – "gladly".

103 *the rabblement hooted* – "the crowd shouted".

104 *nightcaps* – "caps worn in bed and on holidays".

105 *uttered such a deal* – "let out such an amount . . ."

106 *durst* – "dared".

107 *soft* – "stop a moment".

108 *foamed at mouth* – "foam came from his mouth".

109 *'T is very like; . . . falling sickness* – "That is very likely; he suffers from epilepsy".

110 *the falling sickness* – "the illness of being too humble".

Crown

Coronet

yet 't was not a crown neither, 't was one of these coronets

28

BRUTUS

Tell us the manner of it, gentle Casca.[100]

CASCA

I can as well be hanged as tell[101] the manner of it. It was mere
foolery; I did not mark it. I saw Mark Antony offer him a 235
crown, yet 't was not a crown neither, 't was one of these coronets: and, as I told you, he put it by once: but for all that, to
my thinking, he would fain[102] have had it. Then he offered it
to him again; then he put it by again; but to my thinking, he
was very loath to lay his fingers off it. And then he offered it 240
the third time; he put it the third time by, and still as he refused
it, the rabblement hooted,[103] and clapped their chapped hands,
and threw up their sweaty nightcaps,[104] and uttered such a
deal[105] of stinking breath, because Caesar refused the crown,
that it had almost choked Caesar; for he swooned and fell down 245
at it; and for mine own part, I durst[106] not laugh, for fear of
opening my lips, and receiving the bad air.

CASSIUS

But, soft,[107] I pray you! What? Did Caesar swoon?

CASCA

He fell down in the market-place, and foamed at mouth,[108]
and was speechless. 250

BRUTUS

'T is very like; he hath the falling sickness.[109]

CASSIUS

No, Caesar hath it not; but you, and I
And honest Casca, we have the falling sickness.[110]

111 *tag-rag* – Modern English 'rag-tag', i.e. ragged, beggarly.

112 *as they use to do the players* – "as is their custom with the actors".

113 *came unto himself* – "became conscious again".

114 *common herd* – "crowd (of sheep or cattle)".

115 *he plucked me ope his doublet* – "I saw him pull open his coat".

116 *An I had been . . . word* – "If (*An*) I had been a working man and had not taken him at his word (i.e. believed his words and obeyed him) . . ."

117 *he desired their worships . . . infirmity* – "he asked the noble people to believe it was caused by his illness".

a doublet

CASCA

I know not what you mean by that, but I am sure Caesar fell
down. If the tag-rag[111] people did not clap him, and hiss him, 255
according as he pleased and displeased them, as they use to do
the players[112] in the theatre, I am no true man.

BRUTUS

What said he, when he came unto himself?[113]

CASCA

Marry, before he fell down, when he perceived the common
herd[114] was glad he refused the crown, he plucked me ope his 260
doublet,[115] and offered them his throat to cut. An I had been
a man of any occupation, if I would not have taken him at a
word,[116] I would I might go to hell among the rogues. And so
he fell. When he came to himself again, he said, if he had done
or said any thing amiss, he desired their worships to think it 265
was his infirmity.[117] Three or four wenches where I stood, cried
"Alas, good soul," and forgave him with all their hearts. But
there's no heed to be taken of them; if Caesar had stabbed their
mothers, they would have done no less.

BRUTUS

And after that, he came, thus sad, away?   270

CASCA

Ay.

CASSIUS

Did Cicero say anything?

CASCA

Ay, he spoke Greek.

118 *it was Greek to me.* We still use this to mean "I could not understand it", about any language, Greek or not.

119 *are put to silence* – "have been silenced, have lost their positions".

120 *sup* – "have supper".

121 *am promised forth* – "have promised to go out".

122 *and your mind hold* – "and you still invite me (i.e. keep to the same plan)".

123 *Farewell* – "Goodbye".

124 *blunt* – "plain-speaking"; also "not sharp", so here "dull-witted".

125 *quick mettle* – "of a keen mind".

CASSIUS

To what effect?

CASCA

Nay, an I tell you that, I 'll ne'er look you i' th' face again. But 275
those that understood him smiled at one another, and shook
their heads; but, for mine own part, it was Greek to me.[118]
I could tell you more news too; Marullus and Flavius, for
pulling scarfs off Caesar's images, are put to silence.[119] Fare
you well. There was more foolery yet, if I could remember it. 280

CASSIUS

Will you sup[120] with me tonight, Casca?

CASCA

No, I am promised forth.[121]

CASSIUS

Will you dine with me tomorrow?

CASCA

Ay, if I be alive, and your mind hold,[122] and your dinner worth
the eating. 285

CASSIUS

Good, I will expect you.

CASCA

Do so. Farewell[123] both.

[*Exit*

BRUTUS

What a blunt[124] fellow is this grown to be!
He was quick mettle[125] when he went to school.

126 *in execution of* – "in carrying out
. . ."

127 *However he puts on . . . form* –
"however much he pretends to be
slow" (*tardy*, 'late, slow').

128 *is a sauce . . . to digest his words* –
"is a tasty sauce, served along with
the dish of his cleverness, so that
men enjoy eating up and taking
in what he says . . ."

129 *of the world* – "about the way the
world is moving".

130 *Thy honourable metal . . . with their
likes* – "Your noble character
(*honourable metal*) may be changed
(*wrought*) from its own disposition
or sense of values. And so it is
fitting (*meet*) that men of honourable character stay always (*keep
ever*) with men like themselves"
(*wrought*, 'worked', as metal is
'worked' and shaped).

131 *who so firm that cannot be seduced* –
"what man is so firmly fixed in
honour that he cannot be led into
evil ?"

132 *bear me hard* – "dislike me very
much".

133 *In several hands* – "in different
handwritings".

134 *Writings, all tending to* – "written
papers all speaking of . . ."

135 *wherein obscurely . . . glanced at* –
"in which (*wherein*) in a hidden
way (*obscurely*) Caesar's ambition
shall be indirectly spoken of".

136 *seat him sure* – "sit in power as
safely as he can".

CASSIUS

So is he now in execution   290
Of[126] any bold or noble enterprise,
However he puts on this tardy form.[127]
This rudeness is a sauce to his good wit,
Which gives men stomach to digest his words[128]
With better appetite.   295

BRUTUS

And so it is. For this time I will leave you.
Tomorrow, if you please to speak with me,
I will come home to you, or, if you will,
Come home to me, and I will wait for you.

CASSIUS

I will do so. Till then, think of the world.[129]   300

                                                    [*Exit* BRUTUS

Well, Brutus, thou art noble; yet I see,
Thy honourable metal may be wrought
From that it is disposed; therefore 't is meet,
That noble minds keep ever with their likes;[130]
For who so firm that cannot be seduced?[131]   305
Caesar doth bear me hard,[132] but he loves Brutus.
If I were Brutus now, and he were Cassius,
He should not humour me. I will this night,
In several hands,[133] in at his windows throw,
As if they came from several citizens,   310
Writings, all tending to[134] the great opinion
That Rome holds of his name, wherein obscurely
Caesar's ambition shall be glancéd at.[135]
And after this, let Caesar seat him sure,[136]
For we will shake him, or worse days endure.   315

                                                              [*Exit*

1 The same night. Casca describes the great storm and the horrible things that he has seen. He feels that these are signs of some great evil which is coming upon Italy. Cassius believes that these strange happenings are a warning to Rome that one man has grown too powerful. Casca names Caesar as this man; people say, he goes on, that the councillors of Rome intend to offer the crown to Caesar on the following day – he will rule over all the Roman empire except for Italy itself. Cassius declares that, if this happens, he will kill himself. He wishes that the Romans had more strength and pride to deal with Caesar. But perhaps he is speaking to a *willing* slave who will report his speeches to Caesar. Casca promises to join the conspiracy. Cinna comes to fetch Cassius to meet the others. Cassius gives him the letters which Brutus is to find. He and Casca will visit Brutus that night and persuade him to join them. If once Brutus is on their side, people will think their cause is honourable.

2 *even* – "evening".

3 *Brought you Caesar home?* – "Did you go along with Caesar back to his house?"

4 *sway* – "controlled movement".

5 *unfirm* – "not fixed and steady".

6 *rived the knotty oaks* – "split the hard, knotted oak-trees".

7 *To be exalted with* – "trying to lift itself as high as . . ."

8 *civil strife* – "civil war" (among the gods).

9 *more wonderful* – "even more strange than the storm".

10 *Not sensible of* – "not feeling".

11 *put up* – "put into its sheath".

12 *Against* – "just by".

13 *glazed* – "stared". [This word is sometimes given as *glared*, meaning "looked threateningly".]

14 *annoying* – "injuring".

15 *drawn Upon a heap . . . women* – "gathered into a crowd a hundred women looking as terrible as ghosts".

the knotty oaks[6]

36

Scene III. A street.[1]

Thunder and lightning. Enter, from opposite sides, CASCA, *with his sword drawn, and* CICERO.

CICERO

Good even,[2] Casca. Brought you Caesar home?[3]
Why are you breathless, and why stare you so?

CASCA

Are not you moved, when all the sway[4] of earth
Shakes, like a thing unfirm?[5] O Cicero,
I have seen tempests, when the scolding winds   5
Have rived the knotty oaks,[6] and I have seen
The ambitious ocean swell, and rage, and foam,
To be exalted with[7] the threatening clouds:
But never till tonight, never till now,
Did I go through a tempest dropping fire.   10
Either there is a civil strife[8] in heaven,
Or else the world, too saucy with the gods,
Incenses them to send destruction.

CICERO

Why, saw you any thing more wonderful?[9]

CASCA

A common slave – you know him well by sight –   15
Held up his left hand, which did flame and burn
Like twenty torches joined, and yet his hand,
Not sensible of fire,[10] remained unscorched.
Besides – I have not since put up[11] my sword –
Against[12] the Capitol I met a lion,   20
Who glazed[13] upon me, and went surly by
Without annoying[14] me. And there were drawn
Upon a heap a hundred ghastly women,[15]
Transforméd with their fear, who swore they saw

16 *bird of night* – "owl'.

17 *noon-day* – "noon, midday".

18 *When these prodigies . . . meet* – "When these extraordinary and horrible signs (*prodigies*) occur together (*conjointly*) in this way".

19 *are portentous things . . . point upon* – "show that something horrible is to happen to the country (*climate*) they point out (i.e. in which they happen)".

20 *a strange disposéd time* – "a time when strange things seem likely".

21 *after their fashion . . . purpose* – "according to (*after*) their own way of understanding, quite differently from the real meaning (*purpose*) . . ."

22 *This disturbéd . . . walk in* – "This stormy weather is not for walking in".

the bird of night[16]

38

Men, all in fire, walk up and down the streets.   25
And yesterday the bird of night[16] did sit,
Even at noon-day,[17] upon the market-place,
Hooting, and shrieking. When these prodigies
Do so conjointly meet,[18] let not men say
"These are their reasons; they are natural."   30
For I believe they are portentous things
Unto the climate that they point upon.[19]

CICERO

Indeed, it is a strange disposéd time.[20]
But men may construe things after their fashion,
Clean from the purpose[21] of the things themselves.   35
Comes Caesar to the Capitol tomorrow?

CASCA

He doth, for he did bid Antonius
Send word to you he would be there tomorrow.

CICERO

Good night then, Casca. This disturbéd sky
Is not to walk in.[22]

CASCA

Farewell, Cicero.   40

[*Exit* CICERO

Enter CASSIUS

CASSIUS

Who 's there?

CASCA

A Roman.

39

23 *by* – "if I may judge by".
24 *what night* – "what kind of night".
25 *Submitting me . . . unbracéd* – "Taking my chance among the dangers of the night, and with my cloak unfastened in this way".
26 *thunder-stone* – "thunder-bolt".
27 *cross* – "angry"; also "flashing across the sky".

28 *did present myself . . . flash of it* – "placed myself just where its flash was aimed".
29 *part* – "business, duty".
30 *you do want . . . use not* – "either you are without them, or you do not use them".
31 *put on fear . . . wonder* – "seem to be afraid and let yourself be surprised".

CASSIUS

Casca, by[23] your voice.

CASCA

Your ear is good. Cassius, what night[24] is this?

CASSIUS

A very pleasing night to honest men.

CASCA

Who ever knew the heavens menace so?

CASSIUS

Those that have known the earth so full of faults.   45
For my part, I have walked about the streets,
Submitting me unto the perilous night;
And thus unbracéd,[25] Casca, as you see,
Have bared my bosom to the thunder-stone;[26]
And when the cross[27] blue lightning seemed to open   50
The breast of heaven, I did present myself
Even in the aim and very flash of it.[28]

CASCA

But wherefore did you so much tempt the heavens?
It is the part[29] of men to fear and tremble,
When the most mighty gods, by tokens, send   55
Such dreadful heralds to astonish us.

CASSIUS

You are dull, Casca, and those sparks of life
That should be in a Roman you do want,
Or else you use not.[30] You look pale and gaze,
And put on fear, and cast yourself in wonder,[31]   60
To see the strange impatience of the heavens.

32 *from quality and kind* – "acting differently from what we would expect of their character and type".

33 *change, from their ordinance* – "change, quite differently from the way they were in the beginning" (*ordinance*, "first natural order").

34 *pre-forméd faculties . . . monstrous quality.* – "their former kind of nature to something monstrous and abnormal".

35 *infused* – "inspired, filled".

36 *Unto some monstrous state* – "of some horrible thing about to happen".

37 *In personal action* – "when he acts like an ordinary person".

38 *yet prodigious grown* – "but changed into something extraordinary, a sign of something horrible to come" (i.e. changing from an ordinary Roman citizen into a man of great power who may become a dictator).

39 *strange eruptions* – "unusual, and terrible happenings".

40 *like to their ancestors* – "as their fore-fathers had".

41 *woe the while* – "I grieve for this present age (*while*)".

42 *Our yoke . . . womanish* – "Our bearing (*sufferance*) of this oppression (*yoke*) shows that we are weak, as women are".

43 *save* – "except"; Caesar was to have the rank of king everywhere except in Italy.

42

But if you would consider the true cause,
Why all these fires, why all these gliding ghosts,
Why birds and beasts, from quality and kind,[32]
Why old men, fools, and children calculate,   65
Why all these things change, from their ordinance,[33]
Their natures, and pre-forméd faculties,
To monstrous quality;[34] why, you shall find,
That heaven hath infused[35] them with these spirits,
To make them instruments of fear and warning,   70
Unto some monstrous state.[36]
Now could I, Casca, name to thee a man,
Most like this dreadful night,
That thunders, lightens, opens graves, and roars,
As doth the lion in the Capitol,   75
A man no mightier than thyself or me
In personal action,[37] yet prodigious grown,[38]
And fearful, as these strange eruptions[39] are.

CASCA

'T is Caesar that you mean; is it not, Cassius?

CASSIUS

Let it be who it is; for Romans now   80
Have thews and limbs like to their ancestors,[40]
But, woe the while,[41] our fathers' minds are dead,
And we are governed with our mothers' spirits;
Our yoke, and sufferance show us womanish.[42]

CASCA

Indeed, they say, the Senators tomorrow   85
Mean to establish Caesar as a king:
And he shall wear his crown by sea, and land,
In every place, save[43] here in Italy.

44 *deliver* – "set free".

45 *Therein* – "In this" (because a man may choose to die).

46 *Nor stony tower . . . brass* – "neither tower of stone nor walls of hammered brass . . ."

47 *be retentive to* – "hold imprisoned . . ."

48 *life . . . to dismiss itself* – "the living man, when he is weary of the prison bars of this world, can always let himself out".

49 *know all the world besides* – "all the rest of the world can know . . ."

50 *But that* – "except for the fact that . . ."

51 *He were no lion . . . hinds* – "He would not be a lion if the Romans were not as full of fear as deer (*hinds*)".

52 *Those that with haste . . . fire* – "those who intend (*will*) to light a great fire quickly . . ."

53 *when it serves . . . base matter* – "when it serves the purpose as if it were the rubbish to make the fire".

54 *Before a willing bondman . . . indifferent* – "in the presence of one who is glad to be a slave; then I know I shall have to pay for my words. But I wear the armour of honour and the danger of punishment is no matter of fear (*indifferent*) to me".

CASSIUS

I know where I will wear this dagger then;
Cassius from bondage will deliver[44] Cassius.   90
Therein,[45] ye gods, you make the weak most strong;
Therein, ye gods, you tyrants do defeat.
Nor stony tower, nor walls of beaten brass,[46]
Nor airless dungeon, nor strong links of iron,
Can be retentive to[47] the strength of spirit;   95
But life, being weary of these worldly bars,
Never lacks power to dismiss itself.[48]
If I know this, know all the world besides,[49]
That part of tyranny that I do bear   100
I can shake off at pleasure.

[*Thunder still*

CASCA

So can I.
So every bondman in his own hand bears
The power to cancel his captivity.

CASSIUS

And why should Caesar be a tyrant then?
Poor man, I know he would not be a wolf,   105
But that[50] he sees the Romans are but sheep;
He were no lion, were not Romans hinds.[51]
Those that with haste will make a mighty fire,[52]
Begin it with weak straws. What trash is Rome,
What rubbish, and what offal, when it serves   110
For the base matter,[53] to illuminate
So vile a thing as Caesar! But oh grief,
Where hast thou led me? I perhaps speak this
Before a willing bondman; then I know
My answer must be made. But I am armed,   115
And dangers are to me indifferent.[54]

55 *That is no fleering tell-tale* – "who
does not make reports on his
friends like a disloyal flatterer"
(*fleering*, 'flattering'; also 'changing
in purpose').

56 *Hold, my hand . . . As who goes
farthest* – "Say no more (*Hold*); let
us shake hands: if you join in a plot
(*Be factious*) to remedy (*redress*) all
these evils (*griefs*), then I will join
in and help as much as anyone".
Casca keeps this promise; he is the
first to stike Caesar.

57 *know you, Casca, . . . dangerous
consequence* – "let me tell you,
Casca, I have begun to persuade
some of the best and wisest Romans
to risk (*undergo*) with me an adven-
ture (*enterprise*) which will bring
with it both honour and danger".

58 *by this . . . In Pompey's porch* – "that
by this time they are waiting for
me in the entrance to Pompey's
theatre".

59 *the complexion . . . Is feverous* – "the
appearance (*complexion*) of the sky
(*element*) is red like fever . . ."
[This line is sometimes given *In
favour*'s meaning 'In appearance is
. . .']

60 *Stand close* – "Hide here and keep
still".

61 *incorporate To our attempts* – "who
has joined in what we are trying to
do".

CASCA

You speak to Casca, and to such a man
That is no fleering tell-tale.[55] Hold, my hand:
Be factious for redress of all these griefs,
And I will set this foot of mine as far   120
As who goes farthest.[56]

CASSIUS

          There 's a bargain made.
Now know you, Casca, I have moved already
Some certain of the noblest-minded Romans
To undergo with me an enterprise
Of honourable, dangerous consequence;[57]   125
And I do know, by this they stay for me
In Pompey's porch;[58] for now, this fearful night,
There is no stir or walking in the streets;
And the complexion of the element
Is feverous,[59] like the work we have in hand,   130
Most bloody, fiery, and most terrible.

Enter CINNA

CASCA

Stand close[60] awhile, for here comes one in haste.

CASSIUS

'T is Cinna; I do know him by his gait.
He is a friend. Cinna, where haste you so?

CINNA

To find out you. Who 's that? Metellus Cimber?   135

CASSIUS

No, it is Casca, one incorporate
To our attempts.[61] Am I not stayed for, Cinna?

62 *on 't* – "about it" (that Casca has joined them).

63 *look you lay it . . . find it* – "see that you place it in the magistrate's chair where only Brutus will find it".

64 *set this up* – "fasten this".

65 *old Brutus' statue*. The statue of an earlier Brutus who drove out Tarquin, the last king of Rome.

66 *all this done, Repair to Pompey's porch* – "when all this has been finished, come to the porch of Pompey's theatre".

67 *hie* – "hurry on my way".

68 *bestow* – "place".

69 *the man entire . . . yields him ours* – "the whole of Brutus (*the man entire*), when we next meet (*upon the next encounter*), will give himself up to us".

the praetor's chair[63]

48

CINNA

I am glad on 't.⁶² What a fearful night is this!
There 's two or three of us have seen strange sights.

CASSIUS

Am I not stayed for? Tell me.

CINNA

                    Yes, you are.   140
O Cassius, if you could
But win the noble Brutus to our party –

CASSIUS

Be you content. Good Cinna, take this paper,
And look you lay it in the praetor's chair,
Where Brutus may but find it;⁶³ and throw this   145
In at his window; set this up⁶⁴ with wax
Upon old Brutus' statue;⁶⁵ all this done,
Repair to Pompey's porch,⁶⁶ where you shall find us.
Is Decius Brutus and Trebonius there?

CINNA

All but Metellus Cimber, and he 's gone   150
To seek you at your house. Well, I will hie,⁶⁷
And so bestow⁶⁸ these papers as you bade me.

CASSIUS

That done, repair to Pompey's theatre.

                          [*Exit* CINNA

Come, Casca, you and I will yet, ere day,
See Brutus at his house; three parts of him   155
Is ours already, and the man entire,
Upon the next encounter, yields him ours.⁶⁹

70 *he sits high . . . hearts* – "he has a good name with everyone".

71 *appear offence* – "seem to be wrong-doing".

72 *His countenance* – "his approval, and his joining with us . . ."

73 *like richest alchemy* – "like the stone of the alchemists which (it was believed) could turn everything to richest gold". (The alchemists were philosophers and scientists who worked and studied trying to find this stone.)

74 *worthiness* – "honour".

75 *right well conceited* – "very exactly described in this figure of speech about the alchemist".

76 *be sure of him* – "be certain that he is on our side".

CASCA

O, he sits high in all the people's hearts;[70]
And that which would appear offence[71] in us,
His countenance,[72] like richest alchemy,[73]   160
Will change to virtue, and to worthiness.[74]

CASSIUS

Him, and his worth, and our great need of him,
You have right well conceited.[75] Let us go,
For it is after midnight, and ere day,
We will awake him and be sure of him.[76]   165

[*Exeunt*

1 It is the middle of the night. Brutus is debating with himself whether or not Caesar will be an unjust ruler. He has no personal feelings against him but decides that Caesar must die before he can gain absolute power. He reads the letter which his page, Lucius, has found in the window. Remembering how his ancestor drove out the last king from Rome, he promises to save Rome from Caesar. Cassius and the other conspirators arrive. Brutus says that they must not swear an oath; it is enough that their cause is just and they are true Romans. They consider whether or not Cicero shall be asked to join in their plot. Cassius believes that Mark Antony should be killed, with Caesar, but Brutus thinks that Antony will be powerless when Caesar is dead. Cassius is afraid that Caesar may not come to the Parliament House that morning because he has grown superstitious and may be persuaded by the priests to stay at home. Decius says that he will flatter him into coming. When the conspirators have left, Portia comes into the garden. She asks Brutus why he has been so worried and impatient, and what grief he has in his mind. She kneels down before him and asks if she is, indeed, his wife. Brutus promises to tell her all he has agreed to do. Ligarius visits him. Although he is ill, he too will join the conspiracy.

2 *What! Lucius, ho!* – "Come here! Lucius, I want you!"

3 *by the progress. . . day* – "by looking how far the stars have moved on, make a guess how near it is to daybreak".

4 *I would . . . soundly* – "I wish I could be guilty of sleeping so soundly".

5 *When* – "When will you hear me?"

6 *It must be by his death . . . general* – "Only by Caesar's death can Rome be free; and yet, for myself, I have no personal reason for striking him down, only the reason of the general good of Rome" (*spurn*, 'strike down').

7 *would be* – "would like to be".

8 *It is the bright day . . . wary walking* – "It is the sunshine (*bright day*) which brings the poisonous snake (*adder*) from its hole, and that makes it necessary that we step carefully" (*craves*, 'begs').

9 *Crown him that . . . danger with* – "Suppose we crown Caesar as king, then, I agree, we make him like a poisonous snake, able to sting, so that when he pleases he can be dangerous." (The crown given to Caesar would be like the sun's warmth felt by the adder.)

10 *The abuse of greatness . . . power* – "A position of high authority (*greatness*) is misused (*abuse*, 'misuse') when the sense of power cuts off (*disjoins*) kindness and pity (*remorse*)".

ACT TWO

Scene I. Rome. Brutus' Orchard.[1]
Enter BRUTUS.

BRUTUS

What! Lucius, ho![2]
I cannot, by the progress of the stars,
Give guess how near to day[3] – Lucius, I say!
I would it were my fault to sleep so soundly.[4]
When,[5] Lucius, when? Awake, I say! What, Lucius!   5

Enter LUCIUS

Called you, my lord?

BRUTUS

Get me a taper in my study, Lucius.
When it is lighted, come and call me here.

LUCIUS

I will, my lord.

[*Exit*

BRUTUS

It must be by his death; and, for my part,   10
I know no personal cause to spurn at him,
But for the general.[6] He would be[7] crowned.
How that might change his nature, there's the question.
It is the bright day that brings forth the adder,
And that craves wary walking.[8] Crown him that,   15
And then, I grant, we put a sting in him,
That at his will he may do danger with.[9]
The abuse of greatness is when it disjoins
Remorse from power;[10] and, to speak truth of Caesar,

53

11 *I have not known . . . reason* – "I have never known a time when he followed his feelings (*affections*) more than his intelligence" (*swayed*, 'had power').

12 *'t is a common proof . . . face* – "we often find it proved true that an ambitious man, at the beginning of his work in life, climbs the ladder of success by an appearance of humbleness (*lowliness*) and he faces this ladder as he climbs" (i.e. he goes on being humble).

13 *But when . . . round* – "But as soon as ever he reaches the top rung (*upmost round*)".

14 *base degrees* – "low steps".

15 *lest he may, prevent* – "in case he should do this, let us stop it before it happens".

16 *since the quarrel . . . Fashion it thus* – "because our attack (*quarrel*) cannot be excused (*colour*, 'excuse') by what Caesar is at present, let us arrange the argument like this".

17 *augmented* – "if it were made greater".

18 *Would run to these . . . extremities* – "would go as far as this" (i.e. as the misuse of his power).

19 *Which hatched . . . mischievous* – "which, if it were hatched out (i.e. if it grew large enough to break out of its shell), would, as is the nature (*kind*) of all serpents, become dangerous (*mischievous*)".

20 *closet* – "study".

21 *Searching the window . . . flint* – "Looking on the window-ledge for a sharp stone (to get a spark)".

Get me a taper

I have not known when his affections swayed   20
More than his reason.[11] But 't is a common proof,
That lowliness is young ambition's ladder,
Whereto the climber-upward turns his face:[12]
But when he once attains the upmost round,[13]
He then unto the ladder turns his back,   25
Looks in the clouds, scorning the base degrees[14]
By which he did ascend; so Caesar may;
Then, lest he may, prevent.[15] And, since the quarrel
Will bear no colour for the thing he is,
Fashion it thus:[16] that what he is, augmented,[17]   30
Would run to these, and these extremities;[18]
And therefore think him as a serpent's egg,
Which hatched, would, as his kind, grow mischievous,[19]
And kill him in the shell.

Re-enter LUCIUS

LUCIUS

The taper burneth in your closet,[20] sir: 35
Searching the window for a flint,[21] I found
This paper, thus sealed up, and I am sure
It did not lie there when I went to bed.

[*Gives him the letter*

BRUTUS

Get you to bed again; it is not day.
Is not tomorrow, boy, the Ides of March?   40

LUCIUS

I know not, sir.

BRUTUS

Look in the calendar, and bring me word.

55

22 *exhalations* – "meteors or shooting stars".

23 *instigations* – "letters urging me on".

24 *piece it out* – "imagine the rest of it".

25 *awe* – "control, rule".

26 *The Tarquin*. Tarquin was the last king of Rome, and was driven out by an ancestor of Brutus.

27 *thou receivest . . . Brutus* – "You shall have all you ask for from Brutus".

28 *March is wasted fourteen days* – "Fourteen days of March are gone".

29 *within* – "behind the stage".

LUCIUS

I will, sir.

[Exit

BRUTUS

The exhalations[22] whizzing in the air
Give so much light that I may read by them.   45

[Opens the letter, and reads

"Brutus, thou sleepst: awake, and see thyself:
Shall Rome, &c. Speak, strike, redress.
Brutus, thou sleepst: awake."
Such instigations[23] have been often dropped
Where I have took them up: 50
"Shall Rome, &c." Thus must I piece it out:[24]
Shall Rome stand under one man's awe?[25] What, Rome?
My ancestors did from the streets of Rome
The Tarquin[26] drive, when he was called a king.
"Speak, strike, redress." Am I entreated   55
To speak and strike? O Rome, I make thee promise,
If the redress will follow, thou receivest
Thy full petition at the hand of Brutus![27]

Re-enter LUCIUS

LUCIUS

Sir, March is wasted fourteen days.[28]

[Knocking within[29]

BRUTUS

'T is good. Go to the gate. Somebody knocks: 60

[Exit LUCIUS

Since Cassius first did whet me against Caesar
I have not slept.
Between the acting of a dreadful thing
And the first motion, all the interim is

30 *Between the acting . . . phantasma* –
"Between the carrying out (*acting*)
of a terrible deed and the first
thought of it (*motion*), all the time
in between (*interim*) is like a
vision".

31 *The genius . . . insurrection* – "The
inner spirit which controls a man
(*genius*) and those parts of him
which will one day die (*mortal
instruments*) are then in debate
(*council*); and the man can be
compared to a little kingdom
suffering something like (*the nature
of*) a civil war (*insurrection*), with
one part of his mind fighting
against the rest of him".

32 *brother* – "brother-in-law".

33 *moe* – "more".

34 *That by no means . . . favour* – "so
that I cannot at all tell who they
are by any special thing (*mark*) in
any man's appearance (*favour*)".

35 *faction* – "men who have made the
plot".

36 *Shamest thou . . . free?* – "are you
ashamed to show your terrible
face (*brow*, 'forehead') even at
night, when wicked things move
most freely?"

37 *monstrous visage* – "hideous face".

Like a phantasma[30] or a hideous dream.   65
The genius, and the mortal instruments
Are then in council; and the state of man,
Like to a little kingdom, suffers then
The nature of an insurrection.[31]

Re-enter LUCIUS

LUCIUS

Sir, 't is your brother[32] Cassius at the door,   70
Who doth desire to see you.

BRUTUS
Is he alone?

LUCIUS

No, sir, there are moe[33] with him.

BRUTUS
Do you know them?

LUCIUS

No, sir; their hats are plucked about their ears,
And half their faces buried in their cloaks,
That by no means I may discover them   75
By any mark of favour.[34]

BRUTUS
Let them enter:

[*Exit* LUCIUS

They are the faction.[35] O conspiracy,
Sham'st thou to show thy dangerous brow by night
When evils are most free?[36] O then, by day
Where wilt thou find a cavern dark enough   80
To mask thy monstrous visage?[37] Seek none, conspiracy,

38 *it* – "your face".

39 *if thou path . . . prevention* – "if you go on your way (*path*) in your real appearance (*native semblance*), even Hell itself would not be dark enough to hide you from those who would prevent your action".

40 *we are too bold upon your rest* – "we go too far in disturbing your night's rest".

41 *Do we trouble you?* – "Are we being a nuisance to you?"

42 *this hour* – "for an hour".

43 *no man here But honours you* – "there is no man here who does not admire you".

44 *doth wish You had but* – "wishes only that you had . . ."

Hide it[38] in smiles, and affability.
For if thou path, thy native semblance on,
Not Erebus itself were dim enough,
To hide thee from prevention.[39]   85

Enter the conspirators, CASSIUS, CASCA, DECIUS,
CINNA, METELLUS, *and* TREBONIUS

CASSIUS

I think we are too bold upon your rest.[40]
Good morrow, Brutus. Do we trouble you?[41]

BRUTUS

I have been up this hour,[42] awake all night.
Know I these men, that come along with you?

CASSIUS

Yes, every man of them; and no man here   90
But honours you;[43] and every one doth wish
You had but[44] that opinion of yourself,
Which every noble Roman bears of you.
This is Trebonius.

BRUTUS

He is welcome hither.

CASSIUS

This, Decius Brutus.

BRUTUS

He is welcome too.   95

CASSIUS

This, Casca; this, Cinna; and this, Metellus
Cimber.

61

45 *What watchful cares . . . and night?* – "What worries that keep you awake prevent your sleeping at night?" (*watchful*, 'waking'; *interpose themselves*, 'get in the way').

46 *Here lies* – "On this side is . . ."

47 *fret* – "make thin cracks among".

48 *You shall confess . . . the year* – "You will have to admit (*confess*) that you are both wrong. Here, where I am pointing my sword, is where the sun rises, and it is a long way to the south because now it is spring".

49 *Some two months hence . . . here* – "about (*some*) two months from now (*hence*), the sun rises higher towards the north, – and the east, just as the Capitol stands in the most important part of Rome, is here right (*directly*) above our heads".

50 *all over* – "all of you" (i.e. all along the line of men).

62

BRUTUS

They are all welcome.
What watchful cares do interpose themselves
Betwixt your eyes and night?[45]

CASSIUS

        Shall I entreat a word?   100

              [They whisper

DECIUS

Here lies[46] the east; doth not the day break here?

CASCA

No.

CINNA

O pardon, sir, it doth; and yon grey lines
That fret[47] the clouds are messengers of day.

CASCA

You shall confess that you are both deceived: 105
Here, as I point my sword, the sun arises,
Which is a great way growing on the south,
Weighing the youthful season of the year; – [48]
Some two months hence, up higher toward the north
He first presents his fire, – and the high east   110
Stands as the Capitol, directly here.[49]

BRUTUS

Give me your hands all over,[50] one by one.

CASSIUS

And let us swear our resolution.

51 *if, not the face . . . betimes* – "if not even the way men look, the way we suffer (*sufferance*) in our hearts, the evils (*abuse*) of this time – if these are not strong enough reasons (*motives*) let us stop at once (*betimes*)".

52 *high-sighted* – "proud".

53 *range on* – "go freely on".

54 *drop by lottery* – "fall dead as, in the game of chance (*lottery*), his turn comes to be killed".

55 *if these . . . bear fire . . . spirits of women* – "if these reasons . . . have enough feeling in them to make even cowards burn with anger, and to make hard and sharp (*steel*) with courage the hearts of women, which are full of tears and gentleness (*melting*)".

56 *What need we any spur* – "what need have we of any other thing to drive us on . . ." (A spur is a small spike on the rider's heel by which a horse is urged on.)

57 *but our own cause . . . redress* – "except our own purpose to goad (*prick*) us on to find a remedy (*redress*)".

58 *What other bond . . . palter?* – "What other tie (*bond*) to join us together except that (*than*) we are Romans and able to keep a secret, who have made an agreement (*spoke the word*) and will not be dishonest (*palter*)?"

59 *engaged* – "promised".

60 *fall* – "die".

61 *Swear priests* – "Let these men swear, the priests . . ."

62 *men cautelous* – "deceitful men".

63 *suffering* – "long-suffering".

64 *unto bad causes swear . . . doubt* – "When what the men are fighting for is evil, let those who cannot be trusted take an oath".

65 *even virtue* – "justice and strength".

66 *insuppressive mettle* – "force which cannot be held in check".

67 *performance* – "action".

68 *Is guilty of a several bastardy* – "Shows itself not born of a Roman father".

69 *passed from* – "been spoken by . . ."

70 *stand very strong with us* – "give us a great deal of support and help".

BRUTUS

No, not an oath; if, not the face of men,
The sufferance of our souls, the time's abuse, –   115
If these be motives weak, break off betimes,[51]
And every man hence to his idle bed:
So let high-sighted[52] tyranny range on,[53]
Till each man drop by lottery.[54] But if these,
As I am sure they do, bear fire enough   120
To kindle cowards, and to steel with valour
The melting spirits of women,[55] then, countrymen,
What need we any spur[56] but our own cause
To prick us to redress?[57] What other bond
Than secret Romans that have spoke the word   125
And will not palter?[58] And what other oath,
Than honesty to honesty engaged,[59]
That this shall be, or we will fall[60] for it.
Swear priests[61] and cowards and men cautelous,[62]
Old feeble carrions and such suffering[63] souls   130
That welcome wrongs; unto bad causes swear
Such creatures as men doubt;[64] but do not stain
The even virtue[65] of our enterprise,
Nor the insuppressive mettle[66] of our spirits,
To think that or our cause or our performance[67]   135
Did need an oath; when every drop of blood
That every Roman bears, and nobly bears,
Is guilty of a several bastardy,[68]
If he do break the smallest particle
Of any promise that hath passed from[69] him.   140

CASSIUS

But what of Cicero? Shall we sound him?
I think he will stand very strong with us.[70]

CASCA

Let us not leave him out.

65

71 *his silver hairs . . . deeds* – "his age
and white hairs will be like silver
coins to buy us a good name
(*opinion*) as men of honour, and
to win over people to praise
(*commend*) our actions".

72 *Our youths and wildness . . .
gravity* – "That we are young, and
likely to act too quickly and without thinking, will not be realised
at all; it will be covered by
(*buried in*) his seriousness (*gravity*)".

73 *break with him* – "tell him of our
plans".

74 *no man else* – "no other man . . ."

75 *well urged* – "that is a good suggestion".

76 *of him* – "in him . . ."

77 *contriver* – "a man able to act and
plan and do a lot with a little".

78 *his means . . . annoy us all* – "if he
is careful to use all his power
against us, he may be able to do
us great harm" (*annoy*, 'injure').

79 *which to prevent* – "and to stop this
before it happens . . ."

CINNA

No, by no means.

METELLUS

O let us have him, for his silver hairs
Will purchase us a good opinion,   145
And buy men's voices to commend our deeds.[71]
It shall be said his judgement ruled our hands;
Our youths and wildness shall no whit appear,
But all be buried in his gravity.[72]

BRUTUS

O name him not; let us not break with him,[73]   150
For he will never follow any thing
That other men begin.

CASSIUS

Then leave him out.

CASCA

Indeed, he is not fit.

DECIUS

Shall no man else[74] be touched but only Caesar?

CASSIUS

Decius, well urged:[75] I think it is not meet,   155
Mark Antony, so well beloved of Caesar,
Should outlive Caesar; we shall find of him[76]
A shrewd contriver.[77] And you know his means,
If he improve them, may well stretch so far
As to annoy us all,[78] which to prevent,[79]   160
Let Antony and Caesar fall together.

67

80 *the head,* i.e. Caesar.
81 *Like wrath . . . afterwards* – "as if we kill Caesar in anger and then kill Antony out of jealousy".
82 *stand up against* – "fight against".
83 *O that . . . come by* – "if only then we could get at . . ."
84 *their servants,* i.e. our hands.
85 *make Our purpose necessary* – "make what we intend seem necessary".
86 *Which so appearing to the common eyes* – "and if the ordinary people think this . . ."

87 *purgers* – "men who have purified Rome".
88 *for* – "as for".
89 *ingrafted* – "deeply-fixed" (a twig from one tree is *grafted* onto another so that it lives and grows there).
90 *Is to himself . . . company* – "is against himself: he can think of what has happened and die for love of Caesar. And that would be a lot to expect of him, because he is always amusing himself with entertainment, with a gay life and a crowd of friends!"

BRUTUS

Our course will seem too bloody, Caius Cassius,
To cut the head [80] off, and then hack the limbs
Like wrath in death and envy afterwards, [81]
For Antony is but a limb of Caesar.   165
Let us be sacrificers, but not butchers, Caius.
We all stand up against [82] the spirit of Caesar,
And in the spirit of men there is no blood:
O that we then could come by [83] Caesar's spirit,
And not dismember Caesar! But, alas,   170
Caesar must bleed for it. And, gentle friends,
Let 's kill him boldly, but not wrathfully;
Let 's carve him as a dish fit for the gods,
Not hew him as a carcass fit for hounds;
And let out hearts, as subtle masters do,   175
Stir up their servants [84] to an act of rage,
And after seem to chide them. This shall make
Our purpose necessary, [85] and not envious;
Which so appearing to the common eyes, [86]
We shall be called purgers, [87] not murderers.   180
And for [88] Mark Antony, think not of him;
For he can do no more than Caesar's arm
When Caesar's head is off.

CASSIUS

                    Yet I fear him,
For in the ingrafted [89] love he bears to Caesar –

BRUTUS

Alas, good Cassius, do not think of him.   185
If he love Caesar, all that he can do
Is to himself: take thought, and die for Caesar.
And that were much he should; for he is given
To sports, to wildness, and much company. [90]

91 *no fear in him* – "nothing to fear in him".

92 *For he is superstitious grown . . . ceremonies* – "for he has recently begun to believe in signs of good and bad luck, and this belief is quite different from the strong (*main*) opinion he once had about things imagined (*fantasy*) and about dreams and religious sacrifices (*ceremonies*)".

93 *apparent prodigies . . . night* – "hideous signs which have appeared (*apparent prodigies*), the unusual horror (*unaccustomed terror*) of this last night . . ."

94 *o'ersway him* – "make him change his mind".

95 *with trees* – "by means of trees". (It was thought that a man who was trying to catch a unicorn – a one-horned legendary animal – would shelter behind a tree as the animal rushed at him. The horn would then stick in the tree so that the unicorn could not move.)

96 *glasses* – "mirrors". (It was thought that the bear would gaze in the mirror while the man slowly took aim.)

97 *holes* – "pits". (Elephants are caught in pits covered and hidden by branches.)

98 *toils* – "nets or traps".

99 *I tell him he hates flatterers*, implying that Caesar cannot be caught by men who flatter or praise him.

100 *I can give . . . bent* – "I know how to play on his character".

unicorn[95]

TREBONIUS

There is no fear in him;[91] let him not die,   190
For he will live, and laugh at this hereafter.

[Clock strikes

BRUTUS

Peace, count the clock.

CASSIUS

The clock hath stricken three.

TREBONIUS

'T is time to part.

CASSIUS

But it is doubtful yet
Whether Caesar will come forth today or no;
For he is superstitious grown of late,   195
Quite from the main opinion he held once
Of fantasy, of dreams, and ceremonies.[92]
It may be these apparent prodigies,
The unaccustomed terror of this night,[93]
And the persuasion of his augurers,   200
May hold him from the Capitol today.

DECIUS

Never fear that. If he be so resolved,
I can o'ersway him;[94] for he loves to hear
That unicorns may be betrayed with trees,[95]
And bears with glasses,[96] elephants with holes,[97]   205
Lions with toils,[98] and men with flatterers.
But, when I tell him he hates flatterers,[99]
He says he does, being then most flatteréd.
Let me work;
For I can give his humour the true bent;[100]   210
And I will bring him to the Capitol.

71

101 *Nay* – "And more than that . . ."

102 *By the eighth hour . . . uttermost?* – "By eight o'clock. Is that the latest time?"

103 *Be that the uttermost, . . . then* – "Let us agree that that is the latest (We will not wait after eight o'clock), and let us be sure to be there at that time".

104 *doth bear Caesar hard, Who rated him* – "has a deep dislike of Caesar because Caesar scolded him angrily (rated) . . ."

105 *by him* – "past his house".

106 *given him reasons* – "already talked to him of our reasons for hating and fearing Caesar".

107 *send him but hither* – "only send him here".

108 *fashion* – "persuade".

109 *fresh and merrily* – "untroubled and cheerful".

110 *Let not our looks . . . constancy* – "Do not let our expressions (*looks*) show (*put on*) what we intend to do (*our purposes*), but let us act our parts (*bear it*) as our actors do in the Roman theatre, not showing any signs of strain (*with untired spirits*) and not changing our usual serious (*formal*) behaviour", (*constancy*, 'remaining as before').

111 *honey-heavy dew of slumber* – "deep (*heavy*) sleep which drops on your eyes like dew and which is sweet as honey".

CASSIUS

Nay,[101] we will all of us be there to fetch him.

BRUTUS

By the eighth hour; is that the uttermost?[102]

CINNA

Be that the uttermost, and fail not then.[103]

METELLUS

Caius Ligarius doth bear Caesar hard,   215
Who rated him[104] for speaking well of Pompey;
I wonder none of you have thought of him.

BRUTUS

Now, good Metellus, go along by him;[105]
He loves me well, and I have given him reasons;[106]
Send him but hither,[107] and I 'll fashion[108] him.   220

CASSIUS

The morning comes upon 's: We 'll leave you, Brutus,
And, friends, disperse yourselves; but all remember
What you have said, and show yourselves true Romans.

BRUTUS

Good gentlemen, look fresh and merrily,[109]
Let not our looks put on our purposes,   225
But bear it as our Roman actors do,
With untired spirits, and formal constancy;[110]
And so, good morrow to you every one.

[*Exeunt all but* BRUTUS

Boy! Lucius! Fast asleep? It is no matter;
Enjoy the honey-heavy dew of slumber![111]   230

112 *Thou hast no . . . so sound* – "You have no calculations (*figures*), no visions (*fantasies*), which being always worried about the anxieties of the day (*busy care*) seems to produce, as if painting a picture (*draws*), in men's minds; that is why you sleep so soundly".

113 *What mean you?* – "What do you want?" (*mean*, 'intend, want').

114 *for* – "good for . . ."

115 *thus to commit . . . morning* – "to risk getting up like this, when you are not strong, on such a damp, cold morning".

116 *ungently* – "unkindly".

117 *across* – "folded" (a sign of grief and worry in Shakespeare's time).

118 *Yet* – "still, again".

119 *wafture* – "wave".

120 *too much enkindled* – "to blaze up too much".

121 *an effect of humour* – "a result of some disturbance in your mind, some mood". In olden times people believed that a man's character depended upon the four 'humours' – hot, cold, wet and dry – and how they were proportioned in him.

122 *hath his hour with every man* – "takes possession for a time of every man".

123 *could it work . . . condition* – "if it could change your appearance as much as it has changed your character".

124 *dear my lord . . . of grief* – "my dear husband, tell me what is the reason of your sadness".

Thou hast no figures, nor no fantasies,
Which busy care draws in the brains of men;
Therefore thou sleepst so sound.[112]

Enter PORTIA

PORTIA

　　　　　Brutus, my lord!

BRUTUS

Portia! What mean you?[113] Wherefore rise you now?
It is not for[114] your health thus to commit　　　　　235
Your weak condition to the raw cold morning.[115]

PORTIA

Nor for yours neither. You have ungently,[116] Brutus,
Stole from my bed; and yesternight at supper
You suddenly arose, and walked about,
Musing, and sighing, with your arms across;[117]　　　240
And when I asked you what the matter was,
You stared upon me with ungentle looks.
I urged you further; then you scratched your head,
And too impatiently stamped with your foot.
Yet[118] I insisted, yet you answered not,　　　　　245
But with an angry wafture[119] of your hand
Gave sign for me to leave you. So I did,
Fearing to strengthen that impatience
Which seemed too much enkindled,[120] and withal,
Hoping it was but an effect of humour,[121]　　　　250
Which sometimes hath his hour with every man.[122]
It will not let you eat, nor talk, nor sleep,
And, could it work so much upon your shape,
As it hath much prevailed on your condition,[123]
I should not know you. Brutus, dear my lord,　　　255
Make me acquainted with your cause of grief.[124]

75

125 *were he not . . . by it* – "if he were
not well, he would gladly do
what was necessary to regain his
health".
126 *Why, so I do!* In resolving on the
murder of Caesar, Brutus will
bring back health to Rome.
127 *And is it physical . . . unbracéd* –
"And is it a cure to go out without
a cloak . . ."
128 *the humours*–"the mists and dews".
129 *To dare the . . . night* – "to risk
catching an illness from the horrible cold night".

130 *the rheumy and unpurgéd air* – "the
air not yet purified (*unpurgéd*) by
the sun, which will give you a
cough" (*rheum*, 'cough').
131 *some sick offence* – "some sorrow
or wrong which makes you ill".
132 *by the right and virtue of my place* –
"as I am your wife".
133 *incorporate* – "unite".
134 *unfold to me* – "tell me".
135 *heavy* – "full of sorrow and
worry".
136 *Have had resort to you* – "have
come to you".

BRUTUS

I am not well in health, and that is all.

PORTIA

Brutus is wise, and, were he not in health,
He would embrace the means to come by it.[125]

BRUTUS

Why, so I do![126] Good Portia, go to bed.   260

PORTIA

Is Brutus sick? And is it physical
To walk unbracéd,[127] and suck up the humours[128]
Of the dank morning? What? Is Brutus sick?
And will he steal out of his wholesome bed
To dare the vile contagion of the night,[129]   265
And tempt the rheumy and unpurgéd air,[130]
To add unto his sickness? No, my Brutus,
You have some sick offence[131] within your mind,
Which by the right and virtue of my place[132]
I ought to know of; and, upon my knees,   270
I charm you, by my once commended beauty,
By all your vows of love, and that great vow
Which did incorporate[133] and make us one,
That you unfold to me,[134] yourself, your half,
Why you are heavy,[135] and what men tonight   275
Have had resort to you;[136] for here have been
Some six or seven, who did hide their faces
Even from darkness.

BRUTUS

Kneel not, gentle Portia.

77

137 *Is it excepted . . . secrets* – "is there some exception made so that I am not to know all the secrets . . ."

138 *But, as it were . . . limitation* – "only, as one might say, in a way, on some condition . . ."

139 *Dwell I but . . . good pleasure?* – "Is my place only on the outskirts, not in the centre of your love and delight?"

140 *ruddy drops* – "the drops of red blood" (*ruddy*, 'red').

141 *withal* – "in spite of that".

142 *well-reputed* – "of good name" (Cato had a high reputation for courage, honesty and endurance).

143 *Being so fathered, and so husbanded* – "having such a father and such a husband".

144 *counsels* – "plans, discussions".

145 *I have made strong proof . . . husband's secrets?* – "I have tested (*proof*, 'test') my endurance (*constancy*) and shown how strong it is, wounding myself in the thigh of my own choice (*voluntary*). Can I suffer that pain without complaint and not stand the strain of keeping my husband's secrets?"

PORTIA

I should not need, if you were gentle, Brutus.
Within the bond of marriage, tell me, Brutus,   280
Is it excepted I should know no secrets[137]
That appertain to you? Am I yourself,
But, as it were, in sort, or limitation,[138]
To keep with you at meals, comfort your bed,
And talk to you sometimes? Dwell I but in the suburbs   285
Of your good pleasure?[139] If it be no more,
Portia is Brutus' harlot, not his wife.

BRUTUS

You are my true and honourable wife,
As dear to me as are the ruddy drops[140]
That visit my sad heart.   290

PORTIA

If this were true, then should I know this secret.
I grant I am a woman, but withal[141]
A woman that Lord Brutus took to wife.
I grant I am a woman, but withal,
A woman well-reputed,[142] Cato's daughter.   295
Think you I am no stronger than my sex
Being so fathered, and so husbanded?[143]
Tell me your counsels,[144] I will not disclose them.
I have made strong proof of my constancy,
Giving myself a voluntary wound   300
Here, in the thigh. Can I bear that with patience,
And not my husband's secrets?[145]

BRUTUS

                    O ye gods,
Render me worthy of this noble wife!

                                        [*Knocking within*

Hark, hark, one knocks! Portia, go in a while,

79

146 *thy bosom shalt partake* – "your heart shall share . . ."

147 *my engagements* – "my reasons for not taking notice of you"; also "what I have promised to do".

148 *charactery of my sad brows* – "the frowns which have been written on my forehead" (*charactery*, 'writing').

149 *how?* – "how are you?"

150 *Vouchsafe* – "May I say . . ."

151 *a kerchief! Would* – "a shawl (such as sick people put round their shoulders). I wish that . . ."

152 *have in hand* – "is busy with . . ."

153 *Had you a healthful ear . . . of it* – "if you could listen to it with the ears of a healthy man".

And by and by thy bosom shall partake[146]   305
The secrets of my heart.
All my engagements[147] I will construe to thee,
All the charáctery of my sad brows:[148]
Leave me with haste.

                                  [*Exit* PORTIA
            Lucius, who 's that knocks?

Re-enter LUCIUS *with* LIGARIUS

LUCIUS

Here is a sick man that would speak with you.   310

BRUTUS

Caius Ligarius, that Metellus spake of.
Boy, stand aside. Caius Ligarius, how?[149]

LIGARIUS

Vouchsafe[150] good morrow from a feeble tongue.

BRUTUS

O what a time have you chose out, brave Caius,
To wear a kerchief![151] Would you were not sick!   315

LIGARIUS

I am not sick, if Brutus have in hand[152]
Any exploit worthy the name of honour.

BRUTUS

Such an exploit have I in hand, Ligarius,
Had you a healthful ear to hear of it.[153]

LIGARIUS

By all the gods that Romans bow before,   320
I here discard my sickness. Soul of Rome,

154 *derived from honourable loins* – "born of noble ancestors".

155 *hast conjured up My mortified spirit* – "called back by magic (*conjured*) my spirit which was dead (*mortified*)".

156 *strive . . . impossible* – "try to do impossible things".

157 *to do* – "to be done".

158 *whole* – "healthy".

159 *Set on your foot* – "Start on your way".

160 *new-fired* – "full of new energy".

1 Early the next morning. The storm is not yet over. Caesar orders his priests to offer sacrifice to the gods and to let him know if the results are good. Calpurnia begs him to stay at home: too many terrible things have happened during the night. Caesar says that these signs cannot concern him only, but Calpurnia fears they may show that he is soon to die. Caesar answers that brave men cannot fear death; it will come when it must. The servant brings the message that the priests advise Caesar to stay at home: in one of the sacrificed animals there was no heart. Calpurnia begs him on her knees to stay and he agrees. Decius Brutus comes at this moment. Caesar will not send an untrue message that he is ill; he asks Decius to tell the Councillors that he does not wish to come. But, he goes on, because Decius is his friend, he will tell him the true reason. Calpurnia dreamt that she saw his statue running with blood like a fountain, and many Romans were happily bathing their hands in it. Decius keeps his promise to flatter Caesar and explains the dream to mean that Rome shall be strengthened by Caesar's deeds. He tells of the intention of the Senate to crown Caesar as king that day. Are they to say "Not today, but later, when Caesar's wife has better dreams"? Brutus, Antony and the others arrive. Caesar asks Metellus and Trebonius to stand near him on that day. We know how near they are to get to kill him.

2 *night-gown* – "dressing-gown".

82

Brave son, derived from honourable loins,[154]
Thou, like an exorcist, hast conjured up
My mortifiéd spirit![155] Now bid me run,
And I will strive with things impossible,[156]   325
Yea, get the better of them. What's to do?[157]

BRUTUS

A piece of work that will make sick men whole.[158]

LIGARIUS

But are not some whole that we must make sick?

BRUTUS

That must we also. What it is, my Caius,
I shall unfold to thee, as we are going;   330
To whom it must be done.

LIGARIUS

                    Set on your foot,[159]
And with a heart new-fired,[160] I follow you,
To do I know not what; but it sufficeth
That Brutus leads me on.

BRUTUS

                    Follow me then.

                                                        [Exeunt

Scene II. Caesar's house.[1]
Thunder and lightning. Enter CAESAR in his night-gown.[2]

CAESAR

Nor heaven nor earth have been at peace tonight.
Thrice hath Calpurnia in her sleep cried out,
"Help, ho! They murder Caesar!" Who's within?

Enter a SERVANT

83

3 *do present sacrifice . . . success* – "offer sacrifice at once and let me know what they think likely to happen as a result" (*success*, 'a happening which follows').

4 *shall forth* – "intends to go out".

5 *Ne'er looked but on* – "have only seen . . ."

6 *When they shall see . . . vanishéd.* "When I turn and face danger and enmity, all trouble will disappear".

7 *stood on* – "paid much attention to".

8 *fright* – "frighten".

9 *the watch* – "night watchmen, the night 'policemen'".

10 *have yawned . . . dead* – "have opened wide and let out the dead".

11 *and right form of war* – "exactly as if they were fighting a real war".

12 *Which drizzled blood* – "so that blood fell like soft rain . . ."

13 *all use* – "all ordinary happenings".

84

SERVANT

My lord?

CAESAR

Go bid the priests do present sacrifice,   5
And bring me their opinions of success.[3]

SERVANT

I will, my lord.

[*Exit*

Enter CALPURNIA.

CALPURNIA

What mean you, Caesar? Think you to walk forth?
You shall not stir out of your house today.

CAESAR

Caesar shall forth;[4] the things that threatened me,   10
Ne'er looked but on[5] my back. When they shall see
The face of Caesar, they are vanishéd.[6]

CALPURNIA

Caesar, I never stood on[7] ceremonies,
Yet now they fright[8] me. There is one within
Besides the things that we have heard and seen,   15
Recounts most horrid sights seen by the watch.[9]
A lioness hath whelpéd in the streets,
And graves have yawned, and yielded up their dead;[10]
Fierce fiery warriors fought upon the clouds
In ranks and squadrons and right form of war,[11]   20
Which drizzled blood[12] upon the Capitol.
The noise of battle hurtled in the air.
Horses did neigh, and dying men did groan,
And ghosts did shriek and squeal about the streets.
O Caesar, these things are beyond all use,[13]   25
And I do fear them.

14 *Whose end . . . mighty Gods* – "if the gods have decided that it shall happen".

15 *Yet* – "In spite of all these things . . ."

16 *for these predictions . . . as to Caesar* – "since these signs foretelling the future (*predictions*) concern the whole world just as much as they concern Caesar".

17 *blaze forth* – "make known by their flames . . ."

18 *Cowards die many times*, in their imagination.

19 *never taste of death but once* – "only know what it feels like to die when their death occurs". They do not imagine it and fear it before it happens.

20 *an offering* – "a sacrificed animal".

21 *in shame of cowardice* – "to make cowards feel ashamed".

22 *should be* – "would be".

23 *littered* – "born of one lioness". Caesar speaks of Danger as a brother; the two of them are terrible as lions, but Caesar is stronger than Danger.

What say the augurers?

CAESAR

What can be avoided
Whose end is purposed by the mighty gods?[14]
Yet[15] Caesar shall go forth; for these predictions
Are to the world in general as to Caesar.[16]

CALPURNIA

When beggars die, there are no comets seen,   30
The heavens themselves blaze forth[17] the death of princes.

CAESAR

Cowards die many times before their deaths;[18]
The valiant never taste of death but once.[19]
Of all the wonders that I yet have heard,
It seems to me most strange that men should fear,   35
Seeing that death, a necessary end,
Will come when it will come.

Re-enter SERVANT

What say the augurers?

SERVANT

They would not have you to stir forth today.
Plucking the entrails of an offering[20] forth,   40
They could not find a heart within the beast.

CAESAR

The gods do this in shame of cowardice;[21]
Caesar should be[22] a beast without a heart
If he should stay at home today for fear.
No, Caesar shall not. Danger knows full well   45
That Caesar is more dangerous than he.
We are two lions littered[23] in one day,
And I the elder and more terrible,
And Caesar shall go forth.

24 *consumed in* – "eaten up by".
25 *prevail* – "have my own way".
26 *for thy humour* – "because of your mood of fear".
27 *all hail!* – "all good fortune!"

28 *in very happy time* – "at a very fortunate time; just at the right moment".
29 *stretched mine arm . . . afeared* – "fought in lands so far apart and yet am afraid . . ."

CALPURNIA

Alas, my lord,
Your wisdom is consumed in²⁴ confidence.   50
Do not go forth today. Call it my fear
That keeps you in the house and not your own.
We 'll send Mark Antony to the Senate house,
And he shall say you are not well today.
Let me, upon my knee, prevail²⁵ in this.   55

CAESAR

Mark Antony shall say I am not well,
And, for thy humour,²⁶ I will stay at home.

Enter DECIUS

Here 's Decius Brutus; he shall tell them so.

DECIUS

Caesar, all hail!²⁷ Good morrow, worthy Caesar;
I come to fetch you to the Senate house.   60

CAESAR

And you are come in very happy time,²⁸
To bear my greetings to the Senators,
And tell them that I will not come today:
Cannot, is false: and that I dare not, falser:
I will not come today; tell them so, Decius.   65

CALPURNIA

Say he is sick.

CAESAR

Shall Caesar send a lie?
Have I in conquest stretched mine arm so far,
To be afeared²⁹ to tell grey-beards the truth:
Decius, go tell them, Caesar will not come.

89

30 *statuĕ*. Another form of the word *statue*; the last letter, *ĕ*, is pronounced *ay*.
31 *lusty* – "strong and happy".
32 *these does she apply for* – "she looks on these jets of blood as ..."
33 *fair and fortunate* – "good and lucky".

34 *press For tinctures* – "crowd round to get something stained by this blood" (*tincture*, 'colour').
35 *relics*. A bone of a saint would be kept as a holy relic. So Caesar's blood might be kept.
36 *cognizance* – "a mark of honour in a noble's shield".
37 *concluded* – "finally decided".

DECIUS

Most mighty Caesar, let me know some cause,   70
Lest I be laughed at when I tell them so.

CAESAR

The cause is in my will; I will not come.
That is enough to satisfy the Senate.
But for your private satisfaction,
Because I love you, I will let you know.   75
Calpurnia here, my wife, stays me at home:
She dreamt tonight she saw my statuë,[30]
Which like a fountain with an hundred spouts
Did run pure blood, and many lusty[31] Romans
Came smiling, and did bathe their hands in it;   80
And these does she apply for[32] warnings and portents
And evils imminent; and on her knee
Hath begged that I will stay at home today.

DECIUS

This dream is all amiss interpreted.
It was a vision fair and fortunate.[33]   85
Your statue spouting blood in many pipes,
In which so many smiling Romans bathed,
Signifies that from you great Rome shall suck
Reviving blood, and that great men shall press
For tinctures,[34] stains, relics,[35] and cognizance.[36]   90
This by Calpurnia's dream is signified.

CAESAR

And this way have you well expounded it.

DECIUS

I have, when you have heard what I can say;
And know it now: the Senate have concluded[37]
To give this day a crown to mighty Caesar.   95

38 *it were a mock . . . rendered* – "it would be (*were*) a joke (*mock*) they could well make against you . . ."

39 *for my dear . . . proceeding* – "because it is my love for you and my hope of your success (*proceeding*)".

40 *is liable* – "takes second place". (I know I should be wiser not to say this, but because I am your friend I must say it.)

41 *Good morrow* – "Good morning".

42 *are you stirred* – "have you got up . . ."

If you shall send them word you will not come,
Their minds may change. Besides, it were a mock
Apt to be rendered,[38] for some one to say
"Break up the Senate till another time,
When Caesar's wife shall meet with better dreams." 100
If Caesar hide himself, shall they not whisper
"Lo, Caesar is afraid"?
Pardon me, Caesar, for my dear, dear love
To your proceeding[39] bids me tell you this,
And reason to my love is liable.[40] 105

CAESAR

How foolish do your fears seem now, Calpurnia!
I am ashaméd I did yield to them.
Give me my robe, for I will go

Enter BRUTUS, LIGARIUS, METELLUS, CASCA,
TREBONIUS, CINNA *and* PUBLIUS

And look where Publius is come to fetch me.

PUBLIUS

Good morrow,[41] Caesar.

CAESAR

Welcome, Publius. 110
What Brutus, are you stirred[42] so early too?
Good morrow, Casca: Caius Ligarius,
Caesar was ne'er so much your enemy
As that same ague which hath made you lean.
What is 't o'clock? 115

BRUTUS

Caesar, 't is strucken eight.

93

43 *So* – "The same".
44 *call on me* – "speak up and catch my attention".
45 *that* – "so that".
46 *Aside*. Spoken to the audience only (not to Caesar).

47 *earns* – "grieves". Brutus grieves that every 'like' does not mean the same thing. He might be thought to go with Caesar like an enemy rather than like a friend.

CAESAR

I thank you for your pains and courtesy.

Enter ANTONY

See, Antony, that revels long a-nights,
Is notwithstanding up. Good morrow, Antony.

ANTONY

So⁴³ to most noble Caesar.

CAESAR

           Bid them prepare within;   120
I am to blame to be thus waited for.
Now, Cinna, now, Metellus! What, Trebonius,
I have an hour's talk in store for you!
Remember that you call on me⁴⁴ today.
Be near me, that⁴⁵ I may remember you.   125

TREBONIUS

Caesar, I will. [*Aside*⁴⁶] And so near will I be,
That your best friends shall wish I had been further.

CAESAR

Good friends, go in, and taste some wine with me.
And we, like friends, will straightway go together.

BRUTUS

[*Aside*] That every "like" is not the same, O Caesar,   130
The heart of Brutus earns⁴⁷ to think upon.

                        [*Exeunt*

1 Artemidorus has written a warning which he intends to give to Caesar as he passes by on his way to the Capitol. He admires Caesar as a just man and fears the jealousy of Caesar's enemies. This short scene helps to build up fear and uncertainty in the audience: Caesar may be warned in time.

2 *take heed of* – "be careful of . . ."
3 *have an eye to* – "keep a watchful eye on . . ."
4 *mark well* – "watch carefully . . ."
5 *mind* – "intention".
6 *bent* – "aimed (as a bow is bent)".
7 *Security gives way to conspiracy* – "A man who is too confident will

be defeated by those who plot against him".
8 *lover* – "friend".
9 *Out of the teeth of emulation* – "without being torn to pieces by jealous rivals" (*emulation,* 'rivalry').
10 *contrive* – "conspire; work with, in an underhand way".

1 Portia by this time knows of the plans of Brutus and is full of anxiety. It is now nine o'clock and the soothsayer, as well as Artemidorus, intends to warn Caesar.

2 *I would have . . . shouldst do there* – "You would have had time to go there and back again, before (*ere*) I could think of what you should do when you got there".

96

Scene III. A street near the Capitol.[1]
Enter ARTEMIDORUS, *reading a paper.*

ARTEMIDORUS

"Caesar, beware of Brutus, take heed of[2] Cassius; come not
near Casca, have an eye to[3] Cinna, trust not Trebonius, mark
well[4] Metellus Cimber; Decius Brutus loves thee not. Thou
hast wronged Caius Ligarius. There is but one mind[5] in all these
men, and it is bent[6] against Caesar. If thou beest not immortal,   5
look about you. Security gives way to conspiracy.[7] The mighty
Gods defend thee.

                                        Thy lover,[8] Artemidorus."
Here will I stand till Caesar pass along,
And as a suitor will I give him this.
My heart laments that virtue cannot live   10
Out of the teeth of emulation.[9]
If thou read this, O Caesar, thou mayst live;
If not, the fates with traitors do contrive.[10]

                                                          [*Exit*

Scene IV. In front of Brutus' house.[1]
Enter PORTIA *and* LUCIUS.

PORTIA

I prithee, boy, run to the Senate-house.
Stay not to answer me, but get thee gone.
Why dost thou stay?

LUCIUS

                    To know my errand, madam.

PORTIA

I would have had thee there and here again,
Ere I can tell thee what thou shouldst do there.[2]   5
O constancy, be strong upon my side!

3 *O constancy . . . torgue!* – "Let firmness of purpose help me now! Let there be a great mountain between what my heart knows and what my tongue says".

4 *to keep counsel* – "to keep a secret".

5 *For he went sickly forth* – "for he was feeling ill when he went out".

6 *take good note* – "notice carefully".

7 *what suitors press to him* – "what men crowd upon him with their petitions".

8 *a bustling rumour like a fray* – "a noise (*rumour*) of people rushing about (*bustling*) as if there were a fight (*fray*)".

9 *Sooth* – "Believe me".

Set a huge mountain 'tween my heart and tongue![3]
I have a man's mind, but a woman's might.
How hard it is for women to keep counsel![4]
Art thou here yet?

LUCIUS

   Madam, what should I do?   10
Run to the Capitol, and nothing else?
And so return to you, and nothing else?

PORTIA

Yes, bring me word, boy, if thy lord look well,
For he went sickly forth;[5] and take good note[6]
What Caesar doth, what suitors press to him.[7]   15
Hark, boy, what noise is that?

LUCIUS

I hear none, madam.

PORTIA

   Prithee, listen well!
I heard a bustling rumour like a fray,[8]
And the wind brings it from the Capitol.

LUCIUS

Sooth,[9] madam, I hear nothing.   20

Enter the SOOTHSAYER

PORTIA

Come hither, fellow! Which way hast thou been?

SOOTHSAYER

At mine own house, good lady.

99

10 *befriend himself* – "do himself a kindness, look after himself".

11 *know'st thou ... towards him?* – "do you know of any injury which has been planned against him?"

12 *will be* – "*will be* for certain".

13 *chance* – "happen".

14 *Caesar at the heels* – "at Caesar's heels".

PORTIA

What is 't o'clock?

SOOTHSAYER

About the ninth hour, lady.

PORTIA

Is Caesar yet gone to the Capitol?

SOOTHSAYER

Madam, not yet. I go to take my stand,   25
To see him pass on to the Capitol.

PORTIA

Thou hast some suit to Caesar, hast thou not?

SOOTHSAYER

That I have, lady; if it will please Caesar
To be so good to Caesar, as to hear me,
I shall beseech him to befriend himself.[10]   30

PORTIA

Why, know'st thou harm 's intended towards him?[11]

SOOTHSAYER

None that I know will be,[12] much that I fear may chance.[13]
Good morrow to you! Here the street is narrow;
The throng that follows Caesar at the heels,[14]
Of Senators, of Praetors, common suitors,   35
Will crowd a feeble man almost to death.
I 'll get me to a place more void, and there
Speak to great Caesar as he comes along.

[*Exit*

15 *Ay me!* – "Oh, oh!"
16 *speed thee* – "give you success".

17 *Brutus hath a suit . . . grant* – An invented excuse for her words, but the excuse, in fact, proves true. Brutus joins the others to ask that the brother of Metellus Cimber be allowed to return.
18 *commend me* – "give my greetings".

PORTIA

I must go in. Ay me![15] How weak a thing
The heart of woman is! O Brutus,   40
The heavens speed thee[16] in thine enterprise.
[*Aside*] Sure, the boy heard me. Brutus hath a suit
That Caesar will not grant.[17] O, I grow faint!
Run, Lucius, and commend me[18] to my lord,
Say I am merry; come to me again,   45
And bring me word what he doth say to thee.

[Exeunt

1 Both the soothsayer and Artemidorus try to warn Caesar. Brutus and Cassius wait anxiously as the moment for action approaches. Metellus Cimber asks that his brother may be called back from exile. The conspirators kneel before Caesar to second this request. Caesar refuses; Casca, and then the rest, stab him. Antony sends his servant to ask why Caesar has deserved to die. Brutus hopes that Antony may support them; Casca is still afraid of what Antony may do. When Antony arrives in person, and wonders who else is to die, Brutus assures him he is safe; Caesar was killed for the good of Rome. Antony, pretending to accept this reason, asks permission to speak in Caesar's funeral service and Brutus agrees to this. Antony, left alone with Caesar's body, foretells that civil war shall come upon Italy until Caesar's enemies are destroyed and the spirit of Caesar is satisfied.

2 *Hail* – "Greetings".

3 *schedule* – "paper".

4 *o'er-read* – "read through".

5 *At your best leisure* – "when it is most convenient to you".

6 *touches Caesar nearer* – "has to do with Caesar more closely".

7 *What touches us ourself . . . served* – "What concerns me personally shall be dealt with last". Caesar says *us* for *me*, using the 'royal plural', as kings and heads of governments do.

104

ACT THREE

Scene I. Rome. A street in front of the Capitol.[1]
A crowd of people; among them ARTEMIDORUS *and the*
Soothsayer.

Enter CAESAR, BRUTUS, CASSIUS, CASCA, DECIUS,
METELLUS, TREBONIUS, CINNA, ANTONY, LEPIDUS,
POPILIUS *and* PUBLIUS.

CAESAR

The Ides of March are come.

SOOTHSAYER

Ay, Caesar, but not gone.

ARTEMIDORUS

Hail[2] Caesar! Read this schedule![3]

DECIUS

Trebonius doth desire you to o'er-read,[4]
At your best leisure,[5] this his humble suit.   5

ARTEMIDORUS

O Caesar, read mine first: for mine's a suit
That touches Caesar nearer.[6] Read it, great Caesar.

CAESAR

What touches us ourself shall be last served.[7]

ARTEMIDORUS

Delay not, Caesar. Read it instantly.

8 *give place* – "get out of the way".
9 *our purpose is discovered* – "our plan is found out".
10 *makes to* – "goes near to ..."

11 *be sudden . . . prevention* – "be ready to stab Caesar suddenly, for we are afraid we shall be stopped".

CAESAR

What, is the fellow mad?

PUBLIUS

Sirrah, give place. [8]   10

CASSIUS

What, urge you your petitions in the street?
Come to the Capitol.

CAESAR *goes up into the Senate-house, the rest following*

POPILIUS

I wish your enterprise today may thrive.

CASSIUS

What enterprise, Popilius?

POPILIUS

Fare you well.

BRUTUS

What said Popilius Lena?   15

CASSIUS

He wished today our enterprise might thrive.
I fear our purpose is discovered. [9]

BRUTUS

Look how he makes to[10] Caesar. Mark him.

CASSIUS

Casca, be sudden, for we fear prevention.[11]
Brutus, what shall be done? If this be known,   20
Cassius or Caesar never shall turn back,
For I will slay myself.

12 *constant* – "firm in mind".
13 *knows his time* – "knows that the time has come for him to do his part".
14 *prefer his suit* – "speak his petition".

15 *addressed. Press near . . . him* – "ready to do it. Crowd round and join him in this".
16 *throws.* He is ready to throw himself at Caesar's feet.

BRUTUS

Cassius, be constant.[12]
Popilius Lena speaks not of our purposes,
For, look, he smiles, and Caesar doth not change.

CASSIUS

Trebonius knows his time,[13] for, look you, Brutus,   25
He draws Mark Antony out of the way.
                    [*Exeunt* ANTONY *and* TREBONIUS

DECIUS

Where is Metellus Cimber? Let him go,
And presently prefer his suit[14] to Caesar.

BRUTUS

He is addressed. Press near, and second him.[15]

CINNA

Casca, you are the first that rears your hand.   30

CAESAR

Are we all ready? What is now amiss
That Caesar and his Senate must redress?

METELLUS

Most high, most mighty, and most puissant Caesar,
Metellus Cimber throws[16] before thy seat
An humble heart –   35

CAESAR

I must prevent thee, Cimber.
These couchings, and these lowly courtesies
Might fire the blood of ordinary men,
And turn pre-ordinance, and first decree,

109

17 *These couchings . . . of children* – "These kneelings and these humble bows might inflame with pride the hearts of ordinary men, and make them change *(turn)* what had been decided before *(pre-ordinance)*, and alter ancient justice *(first decree)* into a rule in a children's game that could be broken at any time".

18 *fond* – "foolish".

19 *bears such rebel blood* – "has in him a character that rebels against justice".

20 *That will be thawed . . . true quality* – "so that he will be melted from the true and icy justice . . ."

21 *Low-crookéd curtsies . . . spaniel fawning* – "bending low on one knee and humbly flattering like a dog that wants to be stroked".

22 *Know, Caesar doth not . . . satisfied* – "Learn this, that Caesar does not do injustice (the man has been justly banished) and without some good reason Caesar will not be content to change the sentence".

23 *For the repealing . . . brother* – "to ask that my banished brother be allowed to return".

24 *Have an immediate . . . repeal* – "be freed from the sentence and allowed to return at once".

25 *enfranchisement* – "the right to return as a free citizen" *(enfranchisement,* 'freedom from imprisonment or banishment').

26 *I could be well moved . . . move me* – "I could be easily *(well)* persuaded, if I were like *(as)* you; if I could ever ask to stir from the way of justice *(pray to move)*, then your prayers would soften me".

27 *the northern star* – "the Pole star" (by which sailors steer).

28 *Of whose true-fixed . . . firmament* – "which has no equal *(fellow)* in the heavens *(firmament)* for remaining certain and fixed in a known position".

29 *unnumbered sparks* – "points of light too many to be counted".

Into the law of children.[17] Be not fond,[18]   40
To think that Caesar bears such rebel blood[19]
That will be thawed from the true quality[20]
With that which melteth fools, – I mean sweet words,
Low-crookéd curtsies and base spaniel fawning.[21]
Thy brother by decree is banishéd.   45
If thou dost bend, and pray, and fawn for him,
I spurn thee like a cur out of my way.
Know, Caesar doth not wrong, nor without cause
Will he be satisfied.[22]

METELLUS

Is there no voice more worthy than my own,   50
To sound more sweetly in great Caesar's ear,
For the repealing of my banished brother?[23]

BRUTUS

I kiss thy hand, but not in flattery, Caesar,
Desiring thee that Publius Cimber may
Have an immediate freedom of repeal.[24]   55

CAESAR

What, Brutus!

CASSIUS

Pardon, Caesar: Caesar, pardon:
As low as to thy foot doth Cassius fall,
To beg enfranchisement[25] for Publius Cimber.

CAESAR

I could be well moved, if I were as you.   60
If I could pray to move, prayers would move me;[26]
But I am constant as the northern star,[27]
Of whose true-fixed, and resting quality,
There is no fellow in the firmament.[28]
The skies are painted with unnumbered sparks;[29]   65

111

30 *but one ... place* – "only one in all
that number which keeps its
place unchanged."
31 *furnished well* – "well supplied".
32 *apprehensive* – "able to understand".
33 *That unassailable ... am he* – "That
unchanged by any attack (*unassailable*), keeps his noble place
(*rank*), not shaken by any movement; and that I am that man ..."

34 *Olympus.* A mountain in Greece,
the home of the gods, and so
unable to be moved, even by an
earthquake.
35 *bootless* – "without result". 'Even
though Brutus asks this,' says
Caesar, 'I do not grant it. Do you
imagine I will grant it to *you*?'
36 *Speak, hands, for me.* Since *words*
cannot persuade you.
37 *Et tu Brute?* – "Even you, Brutus;
you also?"

They are all fire, and every one doth shine:
But there 's but one, in all, doth hold his place.[30]
So in the world. 'T is furnished well[31] with men,
And men are flesh and blood, and apprehensive;[32]
Yet, in the number, I do know but one   70
That unassailable holds on his rank,
Unshaked of motion; and that I am he,[33]
Let me a little show it, even in this:
That I was constant Cimber should be banished,
And constant do remain to keep him so.   75

CINNA

O Caesar, –

CAESAR

                    Hence! Wilt thou lift up Olympus?[34]

DECIUS

Great Caesar, –

CAESAR

                    Doth not Brutus bootless[35] kneel?

CASCA

Speak, hands, for me.[36]

          [CASCA *first, then the other conspirators and lastly* BRUTUS *stab*
                                                              CAESAR

CAESAR

Et tu Brute?[37] Then fall Caesar.

                                                         [*Dies*

CINNA

Liberty! Freedom! Tyranny is dead!   80
Run hence, proclaim, cry it about the streets.

113

38 *Some to the common pulpits* – "Some go to the platforms from which men speak to the common people".

39 *enfranchisement* – "the right to vote".

40 *affrighted* – "afraid".

41 *Ambition's debt is paid* – "Caesar has died, as he deserved, for his ambition. No one else is to die".

42 *confounded . . . mutiny* – "confused and amazed at this rebellion against Caesar".

43 *fast* – "close, firm".

44 *of standing* – "of our defending ourselves". We do not expect Romans to attack us for what we have done.

45 *good cheer* – "do not be afraid".

46 *should do your age some mischief* – "should injure you, since you are an old man".

114

CASSIUS

Some to the common pulpits,[38] and cry out
"Liberty, freedom, and enfranchisement."[39]

BRUTUS

People and Senators, be not affrighted:[40]
Fly not; stand still. Ambition's debt is paid.[41]   85

CASCA

Go to the pulpit, Brutus.

DECIUS

And Cassius too.

BRUTUS

Where 's Publius?

CINNA

Here, quite confounded with this mutiny.[42]

METELLUS

Stand fast[43] together, lest some friend of Caesar's   90
Should chance –

BRUTUS

Talk not of standing.[44] Publius, good cheer;[45]
There is no harm intended to your person,
Nor to no Roman else; so tell them, Publius.

CASSIUS

And leave us, Publius, lest that the people   95
Rushing on us, should do your age some mischief.[46]

115

47 *abide* – "wait to pay the penalty for" (*abide* has two meanings: 'stay' and 'pay for').

48 *But we the doers* – "except ourselves, who have done this action".

49 *As it were doomsday* – "as if it were the day of judgement".

50 *your pleasures* – "what you decide on for us".

51 *'t is but the time . . . stand upon* – "it is only the latest date and making life last longer that men insist (*stand*) on".

52 *Grant that* – "Once agree on that".

53 *bathe our hands*, as in Calpurnia's dream.

54 *besmear* – "rub the blood on".

55 *walk we forth* – "let us go forward".

116

BRUTUS

Do so, and let no man abide[47] this deed
But we the doers.[48]

Re-enter TREBONIUS

CASSIUS

Where is Antony?

TREBONIUS

Fled to his house amazed.   100
Men, wives and children, stare, cry out, and run,
As it were doomsday.[49]

BRUTUS

            Fates, we will know your pleasures.[50]
That we shall die, we know; 't is but the time
And drawing days out, that men stand upon.[51]

CASCA

Why, he that cuts off twenty years of life,   105
Cuts off so many years of fearing death.

BRUTUS

Grant that,[52] and then is death a benefit.
So are we Caesar's friends, that have abridged
His time of fearing death. Stoop, Romans, stoop,
And let us bathe our hands[53] in Caesar's blood   110
Up to the elbows, and besmear[54] our swords;
Then walk we forth,[55] even to the market-place,
And waving our red weapons o'er our heads,
Let 's all cry "Peace, freedom and liberty!"

117

56 *How many ages hence* – "How many centuries after this . . ." (*age*, 'period of time').
57 *over* – "again".
58 *accents* – "languages".
59 *in sport* – "in play-acting".
60 *on Pompey's basis lies along* – "at the foot of Pompey's statue lies stretched out (*along*)".

61 *knot* – "group".
62 *grace his heels With* – "do him the honour of bringing after him . . ."
63 *Soft* – "Stop a moment".
64 *being prostrate* – "as I lay on the ground at your feet".

118

CASSIUS

Stoop then, and wash. How many ages hence[56]   115
Shall this our lofty scene be acted over,[57]
In states unborn, and accents[58] yet unknown?

BRUTUS

How many times shall Caesar bleed in sport,[59]
That now on Pompey's basis lies along,[60]
No worthier than the dust?

CASSIUS

                              So oft as that shall be,   120
So often shall the knot[61] of us be called,
The men that gave their country liberty.

DECIUS

What, shall we forth?

CASSIUS

                    Ay, every man away.
Brutus shall lead, and we will grace his heels
With[62] the most boldest, and best hearts of Rome.   125

Enter a Servant

BRUTUS

Soft,[63] who comes here? A friend of Antony's.

SERVANT

Thus, Brutus, did my master bid me kneel;
Thus did Mark Antony bid me fall down,
And, being prostrate,[64] thus he bade me say:
Brutus is noble, wise, valiant, and honest;   130
Caesar was mighty, bold, royal, and loving.

119

65 *vouchsafe* – "allow".

66 *resolved* – "told the answer to the problem".

67 *shall not love . . . noble Brutus* – "will give more friendship to the living Brutus than to dead Caesar, and will support and help Brutus . . ."

68 *Thorough . . . untrod state* – "Through the dangers of this new government" (as if in unexplored territory).

69 *true faith* – "loyalty".

70 *so please him* – "if he will".

71 *satisfied* – "given our reasons".

72 *well to friend* – "as our good friend".

73 *have I a mind . . . purpose* – "I cannot help being very much afraid of him, and when I have a feeling that something will go wrong (*misgiving*), my suspicion always (*still*) turns out (*falls*) to have had very good reason".

Say, I love Brutus, and I honour him;
Say, I feared Caesar, honoured him, and loved him.
If Brutus will vouchsafe[65] that Antony
May safely come to him, and be resolved[66]   135
How Caesar hath deserved to lie in death,
Mark Antony shall not love Caesar dead
So well as Brutus living, but will follow
The fortunes and affairs of noble Brutus,[67]
Thorough the hazards of this untrod state,[68]   140
With all true faith.[69] So says my master Antony.

BRUTUS

Thy master is a wise and valiant Roman.
I never thought him worse.
Tell him, so please him[70] come unto this place
He shall be satisfied;[71] and, by my honour,   145
Depart untouched.

SERVANT
I 'll fetch him presently.

[*Exit* Servant

BRUTUS
I know that we shall have him well to friend.[72]

CASSIUS
I wish we may. But yet have I a mind
That fears him much, and my misgiving still
Falls shrewdly to the purpose.[73]   150

Re-enter ANTONY

BRUTUS
But here comes Antony. Welcome, Mark Antony.

74 *Shrunk to this little measure* – "grown so tiny that they need no more space than this".

75 *be let blood* – "have a vein pierced to allow blood to flow from his body so as to cure him of illness". So Caesar has been cured of ambition.

76 *rank* – "grown too large, swollen" (often used of plants and weeds).

77 *bear me hard* – "hate *me* also".

78 *whilst your purpled hands . . . smoke* – "while your hands, dark red with blood, are hot and steaming".

79 *Live* – "If I live . . ."

80 *apt* – "ready".

81 *mean* – "way, method".

82 *by Caesar, and . . . age* – "by the side of Caesar and having my life ended by you, the best and most powerful men of this time".

83 *bloody* – "greedy for blood".

84 *As by our hands . . . act* – "Because of our blood-stained hands and the deed we have just done".

85 *bleeding business* – "act of bloodshed, murder".

86 *pitiful* – "full of pity".

87 *And pity . . . Caesar* – "And sorrow for the injustice (*wrong*) done to the state (*general*) has brought about this action against Caesar, for just as fire defeats fire, so pity for Rome defeated our pity for Caesar." (Fire is used to defeat fire when men burn down houses and trees in the path of a great fire so that it cannot spread further.)

88 *leaden* – soft and blunt as lead.

89 *Our arms . . . you in* – "We take you into our arms, which could otherwise injure you, and into our hearts, as if we were brothers (*malice*, 'power to harm').

90 *good thoughts, and reverence* – "with a good opinion of you (not thinking you a coward or a poor friend to Caesar) and with admiration for you".

91 *In the disposing of new dignities* – "in giving out new honours and positions in the government".

122

ANTONY

O mighty Caesar! Dost thou lie so low?
Are all thy conquests, glories, triumphs, spoils,
Shrunk to this little measure?[74] Fare thee well.
I know not, gentlemen, what you intend,   155
Who else must be let blood,[75] who else is rank.[76]
If I myself, there is no hour so fit
As Caesar's death's hour; nor no instrument
Of half that worth as those your swords, made rich
With the most noble blood of all this world.   160
I do beseech ye, if you bear me hard,[77]
Now, whilst your purpled hands do reek and smoke,[78]
Fulfil your pleasure. Live[79] a thousand years,
I shall not find myself so apt[80] to die.
No place will please me so, no mean[81] of death,   165
As here by Caesar, and by you cut off,
The choice and master spirits of this age.[82]

BRUTUS

O Antony! Beg not your death of us!
Though now we must appear bloody[83] and cruel,
As by our hands, and this our present act,[84]   170
You see we do; yet see you but our hands,
And this, the bleeding business[85] they have done:
Our hearts you see not; they are pitiful;[86]
And pity to the general wrong of Rome –
As fire drives out fire, so pity, pity –   175
Hath done this deed on Caesar.[87] For your part,
To you, our swords have leaden[88] points, Mark Antony.
Our arms in strength of malice, and our hearts
Of brothers' temper, do receive you in,[89]
With all kind love, good thoughts, and reverence.[90]   180

CASSIUS

Your voice shall be as strong as any man's,
In the disposing of new dignities.[91]

92 *be patient . . . multitude* – "wait until we have satisfied and calmed the crowd".

93 *My credit . . . conceit me* – "Your opinion of me (*My credit*) at this time is certain to suffer (as a man on slippery ground is likely to fall) since you are sure to think of me as . . ."

94 *dearer* – "more".

95 *Most noble . . . corse* – "Most noble Caesar, as I stand before your dead body (*corse*)".

96 *It would become . . . enemies* – "It would seem more honourable for me than to join (*close with*) your enemies on terms of friendship".

97 *Here wast . . . brave hart* – "Here, like a brave stag (*hart*) you faced your enemies" (*bayed*, of a hunted deer which has been caught and brought face to face with its enemies just before death).

98 *Signed in thy spoil* – "marked with your blood as if it were a badge of honour" (*sign*, 'to wear like a badge'; *spoil*, 'what is captured in battle').

99 *in thy lethe* – "in your life's blood" (*Lethe*, a river in Hades, the kingdom of the dead; if anyone drank from this river he won eternal forgetfulness).

100 *O world, thou wast . . . heart of thee* – "The whole world was the woodland in which this stag (*hart*) had his kingdom (the empire of Caesar extended over many lands), and the dead Caesar was the centre (*heart*) of the whole world".

Here wast thou bayed, brave hart[97]

124

BRUTUS

Only be patient, till we have appeased
The multitude,[92] beside themselves with fear,
And then we will deliver you the cause,   185
Why I, that did love Caesar when I struck him,
Have thus proceeded.

ANTONY

              I doubt not of your wisdom.
Let each man render me his bloody hand.
First, Marcus Brutus, will I shake with you;
Next, Caius Cassius, do I take your hand;   190
Now, Decius Brutus, yours; now yours, Metellus;
Yours, Cinna; and, my valiant Casca, yours;
Though last, not least in love, yours, good Trebonius:
Gentlemen all, – alas, what shall I say?
My credit now stands on such slippery ground,   195
That one of two bad ways you must conceit me,[93]
Either a coward, or a flatterer.
That I did love thee, Caesar, O, 't is true;
If then thy spirit look upon us now,
Shall it not grieve thee dearer[94] than thy death,   200
To see thy Antony making his peace,
Shaking the bloody fingers of thy foes,
Most noble, in the presence of thy corse?[95]
Had I as many eyes as thou hast wounds,
Weeping as fast as they stream forth thy blood,   205
It would become me better than to close
In terms of friendship with thine enemies.[96]
Pardon me, Julius! Here wast thou bayed, brave hart,[97]
Here didst thou fall, and here thy hunters stand
Signed in thy spoil,[98] and crimsoned in thy lethe.[99]   210
O world, thou wast the forest to this hart,
And this indeed, O world, the heart of thee![100]
How like a deer, strucken by many princes,
Dost thou here lie!

125

101 *Then, in a friend . . . modesty* – "so that it is not too much for a *friend* to say".

102 *pricked* – "marked" (with a dot, the way of marking a list in Shakespeare's time).

103 *Therefore* – "For this reason, because I was willing to be your friend".

104 *Swayed from the point* – "turned away from thinking of friendship".

105 *wherein* – "in what ways".

106 *Or else . . . spectacle* – "If we could not give you such reasons, this would be a cruel sight".

107 *full of good regard* – "full of good sense, of true considerations".

108 *am moreover suitor . . . funeral* – "ask, as one more thing, that I may be allowed to bring his body to the market-place and on the platform (*pulpit*), as a friend should do, speak in his funeral service".

CASSIUS

Mark Antony, –

ANTONY

Pardon me, Caius Cassius: 215
The enemies of Caesar shall say this:
Then, in a friend, it is cold modesty.[101]

CASSIUS

I blame you not for praising Caesar so,
But what compact mean you to have with us?
Will you be pricked[102] in number of our friends,   220
Or shall we on, and not depend on you?

ANTONY

Therefore[103] I took your hands, but was indeed
Swayed from the point[104] by looking down on Caesar.
Friends am I with you all, and love you all,
Upon this hope, that you shall give me reasons,   225
Why, and wherein,[105] Caesar was dangerous.

BRUTUS

Or else were this a savage spectacle.[106]
Our reasons are so full of good regard,[107]
That were you, Antony, the son of Caesar,
You should be satisfied.

ANTONY

                    That's all I seek,   230
And am moreover suitor that I may
Produce his body to the market-place,
And in the pulpit as becomes a friend,
Speak in the order of his funeral.[108]

BRUTUS

You shall Mark Antony.

109 *moved . . . utter* – "stirred to sympathy by what he will say".
110 *By your pardon* – "I am sorry but I think I am right".
111 *protest* – "declare, say".
112 *all true rites* – "everything proper to a funeral service".
113 *It shall advantage . . . wrong* – "It will make the people respect us rather than hate us".

114 *fall* – "happen".
115 *You shall not* – "It is agreed that you must not . . ."
116 *But speak all good . . . of Caesar* – "but say everything good that you can think of (*devise*) about Caesar".
117 *Be it so* – "I agree".

CASSIUS

              Brutus, a word with you.   **235**
You know not what you do. Do not consent
That Antony speak in his funeral.
Know you how much the people may be moved
By that which he will utter?[109]

BRUTUS

             By your pardon.[110]
I will myself into the pulpit first,   **240**
And show the reason of our Caesar's death.
What Antony shall speak, I will protest[111]
He speaks by leave, and by permission:
And that we are contented Caesar shall
Have all true rites[112] and lawful ceremonies.   **245**
It shall advantage more than do us wrong.[113]

CASSIUS

I know not what may fall;[114] I like it not.

BRUTUS

Mark Antony, here, take you Caesar's body:
You shall not[115] in your funeral speech blame us,
But speak all good you can devise of Caesar,[116]   **250**
And say you do it by our permission:
Else shall you not have any hand at all
About his funeral. And you shall speak
In the same pulpit whereto I am going,
After my speech is ended.

ANTONY

             Be it so.[117]   **255**
I do desire no more.

118 *ruins of the noblest man.* He speaks as if Caesar was a great building now in ruins.

119 *in the tide of times* – "in the moving on of time" (*tide*, 'time').

120 *costly* – "precious", *also* "which has to be paid for at a great price".

121 *Which like dumb mouths . . . tongue* – "which, although they cannot speak, seem to open, as if they had lips of rubies, to ask me to use my voice and tongue in speaking for them".

122 *light* – "fall".

123 *Domestic fury . . . cumber* – "Savage fighting among the people of our home and violent civil war shall overthrow (*cumber*) . . ."

124 *in use* – "ordinary".

125 *objects* – "sights".

126 *quartered* – "cut into (four pieces".

127 *All pity choked . . . deeds* – "all pity deadened because people have grown so used to cruelty" (*fell*, 'cruel').

128 *And Caesar's spirit . . . dogs of war* – "And Caesar's ghost, roaming the world (*ranging*) for vengeance, with the goddess of mischief (*Atè*) with him, come fresh (*hot*) from Hell, shall, inside the boundaries of Italy (*these confines*), with the voice of a king, cry out 'Destruction!' (*Havoc*) and let loose (*let slip*) the savage dogs of war".

129 *That this foul deed . . . burial* – "so that this evil murder (*foul deed*), along with other corpses (*carrion men*), shall spread the smell of death and cry out for the burial of many dead." Many more must die before the spirit of Caesar is satisfied.

BRUTUS

Prepare the body then, and follow us.

[*Exeunt all but* ANTONY

ANTONY

O pardon me, thou bleeding piece of earth,
That I am meek and gentle with these butchers.
Thou art the ruins of the noblest man[118]   260
That ever livéd in the tide of times.[119]
Woe to the hand that shed this costly[120] blood!
Over thy wounds now do I prophesy, –
Which like dumb mouths do ope their ruby lips,
To beg the voice and utterance of my tongue –[121]   265
A curse shall light[122] upon the limbs of men;
Domestic fury and fierce civil strife
Shall cumber[123] all the parts of Italy;
Blood and destruction shall be so in use,[124]
And dreadful objects[125] so familiar,   270
That mothers shall but smile when they behold
Their infants quartered[126] with the hands of war,
All pity choked with custom of fell deeds;[127]
And Caesar's spirit ranging for revenge,
With Até by his side, come hot from hell,   275
Shall in these confines, with a monarch's voice,
Cry "Havoc!" and let slip the dogs of war,[128]
That this foul deed shall smell above the earth
With carrion men, groaning for burial.[129]

Enter Octavius's Servant

You serve Octavius Caesar, do you not?   280

SERVANT

I do, Mark Antony.

131

130 *big* – "full of tears which must be shed" (*big*, 'ready to give birth').

131 *Passion* – "Feeling, sorrow".

132 *He lies tonight . . . Rome* – "He intends to lodge (*lie*) tonight less than (*within*) twenty-one miles from Rome" (*league*, about three miles).

133 *Post back with speed* – "Ride back quickly with this message".

134 *Hie hence* – "Go from here quickly".

135 *Yet* – "But, on second thoughts".

136 *borne this corse* – "carried this body".

137 *try* – "test".

138 *take The cruel issue . . . hand* – "accept the cruel deed which these bloodthirsty men have done, and, according to the way they take it, you shall tell young Octavius how things are in Rome. Help me to carry the body".

ANTONY

Caesar did write for him to come to Rome.

SERVANT

He did receive his letters, and is coming,
And bid me say to you by word of mouth –
O Caesar!   285

ANTONY

Thy heart is big;[130] get thee apart and weep.
Passion[131] I see is catching, for mine eyes,
Seeing those beads of sorrow stand in thine,
Began to water. Is thy Master coming?

SERVANT

He lies tonight within seven leagues of Rome.[132]   290

ANTONY

Post back with speed![133] And tell him what hath chanced:
Here is a mourning Rome, a dangerous Rome,
No Rome of safety for Octavius yet.
Hie hence,[134] and tell him so. Yet[135] stay awhile;
Thou shalt not back till I have borne this corse[136]   295
Into the market-place. There shall I try[137]
In my oration, how the people take
The cruel issue of these bloody men,
According to the which, thou shalt discourse
To young Octavius of the state of things.   300
Lend me your hand.[138]

[Exeunt carrying Caesar's body

1 Brutus speaks to the people neatly, clearly, rhythmically and reasonably – in prose; he loved Caesar but slew him for his ambition. The people show how little they understand Brutus by saying of him 'Let him be Caesar'. Antony speaks in verse, feeling his way forward until he can make a direct attack on the conspirators. He appeals to the reason of the crowd: Caesar is charged with ambition, but what he won in war he gave to Rome. He sympathised with the poor in time of famine; three times he refused the crown. Then Antony appeals to the emotions of the people – he breaks off his speech in real grief. He appeals also to their gratitude – he is to read Caesar's will. But before this he looks at the holes torn in Caesar's mantle, a mantle Caesar wore for the first time after his most famous victory. He is no orator but, if he were an eloquent speaker, he would move the very stones of Rome to mutiny. The will is read; the people rush away to burn and kill. Antony goes to meet Octavius: they must take the opportunities which fortune offers.

2 *give me audience* – "listen to me".

3 *part the numbers* – "divide the crowd, take half the people with you".

4 *public reasons . . . death* – "reasons shall be given why Caesar's death was for the good of the state (*public*)".

5 *severally* – "separately".

6 *till the last* – "until I have finished".

7 *countrymen, and lovers . . . my cause* – "men of my country, and my friends, listen to me for the sake of what I believe in".

8 *Believe me for mine honour . . . that* – "Believe me, because otherwise you dishonour me, and think that I am a man of honour so that . . ."

9 *Censure me . . . your senses* – "Judge me according to your good sense and be critical and keen in mind . . ."

Scene II. The Forum.[1]
Enter BRUTUS *and* CASSIUS, *with a crowd of* Plebeians.

PLEBEIANS

We will be satisfied; let us be satisfied.

BRUTUS

Then follow me, and give me audience,[2] friends.
Cassius, go you into the other street,
And part the numbers:[3]
Those that will hear me speak, let them stay here;   5
Those that will follow Cassius, go with him,
And public reasons shall be rendered
Of Caesar's death.[4]

I PLEBEIAN

I will hear Brutus speak.

2 PLEBEIAN

I will hear Cassius, and compare their reasons,
When severally[5] we hear them rendered.   10

> [*Exit* CASSIUS *with some of the* Plebeians;
> BRUTUS *goes into the pulpit*

3 PLEBEIAN

The noble Brutus is ascended. Silence!

BRUTUS

Be patient till the last.[6]
Romans, countrymen, and lovers, hear me for my cause,[7] and
be silent, that you may hear. Believe me for mine honour, and
have respect to mine honour, that[8] you may believe. Censure   15
me in your wisdom, and awake your senses,[9] that you may the

135

10 *As* – "In so far as .."

11 *fortunate* – "successful (in war)".

12 *Who is here so base . . . offended* – "Which man here is so mean-spirited (*base*) that he would choose to be a slave? If there is anyone here who would, let him speak for I have injured (*offended*) him".

13 *rude* – "uncivilised".

14 *The question . . . enforced* – "The reasons (*question*) for his death are written down (*enrolled*) in the Government House (*Capitol*), his noble deeds (*glory*) not made to seem less (*extenuated*), nor his wrong actions (*offences*) described with special force and made to seem greater (*enforced*)".

15 *receive the benefit of his dying* – "have this advantage from Caesar's death".

16 *With this I depart* – "I say this to you as I go . . ."

17 *lover* – "friend".

better judge. If there be any in this assembly, any dear friend of Caesar's, to him I say, that Brutus' love to Caesar was no less than his. If then, that friend demand why Brutus rose against Caesar, this is my answer: Not that I loved Caesar less, but 20 that I loved Rome more. Had you rather Caesar were living, and die all slaves, than that Caesar were dead, to live all free men? As[10] Caesar loved me, I weep for him; as he was fortu-nate,[11] I rejoice at it; as he was valiant, I honour him; but, as he was ambitious, I slew him. There is tears for his love: joy for his 25 fortune: honour for his valour: and death for his ambition. Who is here so base that would be a bondman? If any, speak, for him have I offended.[12] Who is here so rude[13] that would not be a Roman? If any, speak, for him have I offended. Who is here so vile that will not love his country? If any, speak, for him have I 30 offended. I pause for a reply.

ALL

None, Brutus, none.

BRUTUS

Then none have I offended. I have done no more to Caesar than you shall do to Brutus. The question of his death is enrolled in the Capitol, his glory not extenuated, wherein he was worthy, 35 nor his offences enforced,[14] for which he suffered death.

Enter MARK ANTONY *and others, with Caesar's body*

Here comes his body, mourned by Mark Antony who, though he had no hand in his death, shall receive the benefit of his dying,[15] a place in the Commonwealth, – as which of you shall not? With this I depart,[16] – that, as I slew my best lover[17] for 40 the good of Rome, I have the same dagger for myself, when it shall please my country to need my death.

ALL

Live, Brutus, live, live!

18 *Bring him with triumph* – "Let us follow him in a procession of honour".

19 *with* – "among those of . . ."

20 *parts* – "characteristics".

21 *grace* – "honour".

22 *Tending to* – "speaking about"

1 PLEBEIAN

Bring him with triumph[18] home unto his house.

2 PLEBEIAN

Give him a statue with[19] his ancestors.   45

3 PLEBEIAN

Let him be Caesar!

4 PLEBEIAN
     Caesar's better parts[20]
Shall be crowned in Brutus.

1 PLEBEIAN

We 'll bring him to his house
With shouts and clamours.

BRUTUS

My countrymen, –

2 PLEBEIAN
     Peace! Silence! Brutus speaks.   50

1 PLEBEIAN

Peace, ho!

BRUTUS

Good countrymen, let me depart alone,
And, for my sake, stay here with Antony.
Do grace[21] to Caesar's corpse, and grace his speech
Tending to[22] Caesar's glories, which Mark Antony,   55
By our permission, is allowed to make.
I do entreat you, not a man depart
Save I alone, till Antony have spoke.

             [*Exit*

23 *public chair* – "speaker's chair".
24 *For Brutus' sake . . . to you* – "It is because Brutus has asked you to listen that I have to thank you for staying".

25 *beholding to us* – "grateful to us".
26 *Nay* – "No, even more . . ."
27 *blest* – "lucky".
28 *gentle* – "noble and kind".

I PLEBEIAN

Stay, ho, and let us hear Mark Antony!

3 PLEBEIAN

Let him go up into the public chair.²³   60
We 'll hear him. Noble Antony, go up.

ANTONY

For Brutus' sake I am beholding to you.²⁴

[Goes into the pulpit

4 PLEBEIAN

What does he say of Brutus?

3 PLEBEIAN

                    He says, for Brutus' sake
He finds himself beholding to us²⁵ all.

4 PLEBEIAN

'T were best he speak no harm of Brutus here!   65

I PLEBEIAN

This Caesar was a tyrant.

3 PLEBEIAN

                Nay,²⁶ that 's certain;
We are blest²⁷ that Rome is rid of him.

2 PLEBEIAN

Peace! Let us hear what Antony can say.

ANTONY

You gentle²⁸ Romans, –

29 *grievous* – "very serious".

30 *grievously* – "at great cost to himself".

31 *answered* – "paid for".

32 *just* – "loyal, honourable".

33 *Whose ransoms . . . fill* – "and the money they paid for their release went to the state, not to Caesar".

34 *have cried*, in time of famine for lack of food.

35 *What cause . . . for him?* – "What reason stops you then from grieving for his death?"

36 *O judgement! Thou . . . beasts* – "Good judgement, you have fled (from men) to brute beasts!"

142

ALL

Peace ho, let us hear him!

ANTONY

Friends, Romans, countrymen, lend me your ears.   70
I come to bury Caesar, not to praise him.
The evil that men do lives after them;
The good is oft interréd with their bones,
So let it be with Caesar. The noble Brutus
Hath told you Caesar was ambitious.   75
If it were so, it was a grievous[29] fault,
And grievously[30] hath Caesar answered[31] it.
Here, under leave of Brutus, and the rest, –
For Brutus is an honourable man,
So are they all; all honourable men, –   80
Come I to speak in Caesar's funeral.
He was my friend, faithful, and just[32] to me;
But Brutus says he was ambitious,
And Brutus is an honourable man.
He hath brought many captives home to Rome,   85
Whose ransoms did the general coffers fill:[33]
Did this in Caesar seem ambitious?
When that the poor have cried,[34] Caesar hath wept.
Ambition should be made of sterner stuff,
Yet Brutus says he was ambitious,   90
And Brutus is an honourable man.
You all did see that, on the Lupercal,
I thrice presented him a kingly crown,
Which he did thrice refuse. Was this ambition?
Yet Brutus says he was ambitious,   95
And, sure, he is an honourable man.
I speak not to disprove what Brutus spoke,
But here I am, to speak what I do know.
You all did love him once, not without cause;
What cause withholds you then to mourn for him?[35]   100
O judgement! Thou art fled to brutish beasts,[36]

143

37 *Bear with me* – "Be patient with me (I am too upset to go on speaking of this)".

38 *Methinks there is . . . his sayings* – "It seems to me that there is a lot of good sense in what he says".

39 *wrong* – "injustice done to him".

40 *masters* – "men, friends".

41 *a worse* – "a worse evil, a worse ruler".

42 *dear abide it* – "pay a heavy price".

43 *But yesterday . . . world* – "Only yesterday, even if all the world had said no to it, any order given by Caesar would have been carried out".

144

And men have lost their reason! Bear with me,[37]
My heart is in the coffin there with Caesar,
And I must pause, till it come back to me.

1 PLEBEIAN

Methinks there is much reason in his sayings.[38]   105

2 PLEBEIAN

If thou consider rightly of the matter,
Caesar has had great wrong.[39]

3 PLEBEIAN

Has he, masters?[40]
I fear there will a worse[41] come in his place.

4 PLEBEIAN

Marked ye his words? He would not take the crown,   110
Therefore 't is certain, he was not ambitious.

1 PLEBEIAN

If it be found so, some will dear abide it.[42]

2 PLEBEIAN

Poor soul, his eyes are red as fire with weeping.

3 PLEBEIAN

There 's not a nobler man in Rome than Antony.

4 PLEBEIAN

Now mark him; he begins again to speak.   115

ANTONY

But yesterday the word of Caesar might
Have stood against the world;[43] now lies he there,

44 *none so poor to do him reverence* – "every living man is better than Caesar; no one is so poor that he need bow down before him (*do him reverence*)".

45 *closet* – "study, writing-room".

46 *Let but the commons . . . testament* – "if the common people should only hear what Caesar has left in his will . . ."

47 *napkins* – "handkerchiefs".

48 *a hair of him for memory* – "one of his hairs so that they might remember him by it". (Compare this with the interpretation Decius gave to Calpurnia's dream.)

49 *Unto their issue* – "to their children".

50 *I must not* – "It is not right for me . . ."

And none so poor to do him reverence.[44]
O, masters, if I were disposed to stir
Your hearts and minds to mutiny and rage,   120
I should do Brutus wrong, and Cassius wrong,
Who, you all know, are honourable men.
I will not do them wrong; I rather choose
To wrong the dead, to wrong myself and you,
Than I will wrong such honourable men.   125
But here 's a parchment, with the seal of Caesar;
I found it in his closet;[45] 't is his will;
Let but the commons hear this testament,[46]
Which, pardon me, I do not mean to read,
And they would go and kiss dead Caesar's wounds,   130
And dip their napkins[47] in his sacred blood,
Yea, beg a hair of him for memory,[48]
And dying, mention it within their wills,
Bequeathing it as a rich legacy
Unto their issue.[49]   135

4 PLEBEIAN

We 'll hear the will; read it, Mark Antony.

ALL

The will, the will! We will hear Caesar's will.

ANTONY

Have patience, gentle friends; I must not[50] read it.
It is not meet you know how Caesar loved you.
You are not wood, you are not stones, but men;   140
And being men, hearing the will of Caesar,
It will inflame you, it will make you mad.
'T is good you know not that you are his heirs,
For if you should, O what would come of it?

4 PLEBEIAN

Read the will! We 'll hear it, Antony: 145
You shall read us the will, Caesar's will.

147

51 *o'ershot myself* – "gone too far,
shot too far ahead".

ANTONY

Will you be patient? Will you stay awhile?
I have o'ershot myself[51] to tell you of it;
I fear I wrong the honourable men
Whose daggers have stabbed Caesar; I do fear it.   150

4 PLEBEIAN

They were traitors. Honourable men!

ALL

The will, the testament!

2 PLEBEIAN

They were villains, murderers! The will, read the will!

ANTONY

You will compel me then to read the will?
Then make a ring about the corpse of Caesar,   155
And let me show you him that made the will.
Shall I descend? And will you give me leave?

ALL

Come down.

2 PLEBEIAN

    Descend.

              [*He comes down from the pulpit*

3 PLEBEIAN

You shall have leave.

4 PLEBEIAN

A ring! Stand round!

52 *bear back* – "move or push backwards".

53 *mantle* – "cloak".

54 *the Nervii*. A warlike people of N.W. Europe, conquered by Caesar. In the great battle against them, the Roman army, almost defeated, was saved mainly by Caesar's courage.

55 *plucked his curséd steel . . . or no* – "drew out (*plucked*) his evil dagger (*curséd steel*), see how Caesar's blood flowed after it, as if hurrying out of its house to find out (*be resolved*) whether it was indeed Brutus who, so unlike a friend, knocked on the door (i.e. stabbed Caesar's body)".

56 *angel* – "darling".

57 *the most unkindest cut* – "the blow which hurt Caesar most".

58 *Ingratitude . . . fell* – "the thought that Brutus was so ungrateful to him (*Ingratitude*) was worse than the swords of the conspirators, and ended his resistance (*quite vanquished him*); then his great heart broke (*burst*), and covering his face with his cloak, he fell down just (*even*) at the foot (*base*) of Pompey's statue, which all this time was flowing with (*ran*) blood".

I PLEBEIAN

Stand from the hearse; stand from the body!   160

2 PLEBEIAN

Room for Antony, most noble Antony!

ANTONY

Nay, press not so upon me; stand far off.

ALL

Stand back; room, bear back!⁵²

ANTONY

If you have tears, prepare to shed them now.
You all do know this mantle.⁵³ I remember   165
The first time ever Caesar put it on.
'T was on a summer's evening in his tent,
That day he overcame the Nervii.⁵⁴
Look, in this place ran Cassius' dagger through;
See what a rent the envious Casca made;   170
Through this, the well-belovéd Brutus stabbed,
And, as he plucked his curséd steel away,
Mark how the blood of Caesar followed it,
As rushing out of doors, to be resolved
If Brutus so unkindly knocked, or no;⁵⁵   175
For Brutus, as you know, was Caesar's angel.⁵⁶
Judge, O you gods, how dearly Caesar loved him!
This was the most unkindest cut⁵⁷ of all.
For when the noble Caesar saw him stab,
Ingratitude, more strong than traitors' arms,   180
Quite vanquished him; then burst his mighty heart,
And in his mantle muffling up his face,
Even at the base of Pompey's statuë,
Which all the while ran blood, great Caesar fell.⁵⁸
O what a fall was there, my countrymen!   185

59 *fell down, Whilst . . . over us* – "lost our freedom while murderous men, betraying their country (*bloody treason*), grew powerful (*flourished*) over us".

60 *dint* – "hard blow".

61 *gracious* – "showing sympathy".

62 *Kind souls . . . traitors* – "Kind hearts, why (*what*) do you cry when you see only the *clothing* of Caesar torn or wounded? Here is Caesar himself hurt (*marred*) by those men who betrayed him".

63 *About, seek* – "Let us go through the whole city and look for the criminals".

Then I, and you, and all of us fell down,
Whilst bloody treason flourished over us.[59]
O now you weep, and I perceive you feel
The dint[60] of pity. These are gracious[61] drops.
Kind souls, what weep you, when you but behold   190
Our Caesar's vesture wounded? Look you here!
Here is himself, marred, as you see, with traitors.[62]

1 PLEBEIAN

O piteous spectacle!

2 PLEBEIAN

O noble Caesar!

3 PLEBEIAN

O woeful day!   195

4 PLEBEIAN

O traitors, villains!

1 PLEBEIAN

O most bloody sight!

2 PLEBEIAN

We will be revenged! Revenge,
About, seek,[63] burn, fire, kill, slay!
Let not a traitor live!   200

ANTONY

Stay, countrymen!

1 PLEBEIAN

Peace, there! Hear the noble Antony.

2 PLEBEIAN

We 'll hear him, we 'll follow him, we 'll die with him!

64 *To such a sudden flood of mutiny* –
"to move to rebellion like a sudden
flood or tide".

65 *private griefs* – "personal reasons for
disliking Caesar".

66 *That gave me . . . him* – "those who
gave me permission to speak of him
in public".

67 *writ, nor words . . . right on* – "permission (*writ*), nor fine words, nor
personal merit (*worth*), nor the
gestures of an actor (*action*), nor
the way of speaking (*utterance*),
nor skill in putting words together
(*power of speech*), to move men's
feelings. I only say just what comes
into my head (*right on*)".

68 *dumb mouths* – "open wounds,
which, although they cannot speak,
ask for pity".

69 *were I Brutus . . . wound of Caesar* –
"if I were Brutus, and if Brutus
were myself now speaking to you,
then you would certainly hear
someone who could rouse your
hearts and make Caesar's wounds
speak to you".

ANTONY

Good friends, sweet friends, let me not stir you up
To such a sudden flood of mutiny.[64]   205
They that have done this deed are honourable.
What private griefs[65] they have, alas, I know not,
That made them do it; they are wise, and honourable,
And will, no doubt, with reasons answer you.
I come not, friends, to steal away your hearts;   210
I am no orator, as Brutus is.
But, as you know me all, a plain blunt man
That love my friend; and that they know full well,
That gave me public leave to speak of him;[66]
For I have neither writ, nor words, nor worth,   215
Action, nor utterance, nor the power of speech,
To stir men's blood. I only speak right on.[67]
I tell you that which you yourselves do know,
Show you sweet Caesar's wounds, poor, poor dumb mouths,[68]
And bid them speak for me; but were I Brutus,   220
And Brutus Antony, there were an Antony
Would ruffle up your spirits, and put a tongue
In every wound of Caesar,[69] that should move
The stones of Rome to rise and mutiny.

ALL

We 'll mutiny.

I PLEBEIAN

We 'll burn the house of Brutus.   225

3 PLEBEIAN

Away then, come, seek the conspirators!

ANTONY

Yet hear me, countrymen, yet hear me speak.

70 *Wherein* – "in what way, for what reasons?"

71 *under* – "marked with".

72 *To every . . . drachmas* – "to each man separately £3" (*drachma*, a silver coin worth tenpence, so that 75 drachmas was worth about £3).

73 *Moreover, he hath left . . . Tiber* – "In addition, he has left you all his gardens (*walks*), his own summer-houses (*private arbours*) and freshly-planted orchards on this side of the river Tiber".

74 *common pleasures . . . recreate yourselves* – "pleasure gardens for you all (*common pleasures*), where you may walk in the open air (*abroad*) to rest and enjoy (*recreate*) yourselves".

75 *Here was a Caesar . . . another?* – "This was a great ruler. When will there be another like him?"

ALL

Peace, ho, hear Antony, most noble Antony!

ANTONY

Why, friends, you go to do you know not what.
Wherein[70] hath Caesar thus deserved your loves?   230
Alas, you know not. I must tell you then;
You have forgot the will I told you of.

ALL

Most true; the will; let 's stay and hear the will!

ANTONY

Here is the will, and under[71] Caesar's seal:
To every Roman citizen he gives,   235
To every several man, seventy-five drachmas.[72]

2 PLEBEIAN

Most noble Caesar! We 'll revenge his death.

3 PLEBEIAN

O royal Caesar!

ANTONY

Hear me with patience.

ALL

Peace, ho!   240

ANTONY

Moreover, he hath left you all his walks,
His private arbours and new-planted orchards,
On this side Tiber;[73] he hath left them you,
And to your heirs for ever, common pleasures
To walk abroad, and recreate yourselves.[74]   245
Here was a Caesar! When comes such another?[75]

157

76 *the holy place*, the Forum, centre of
religious life in Rome.

77 *with the brands . . . houses* – "with
pieces of burning wood from
Caesar's funeral pyre, we will set
on fire the houses of those who
betrayed him".

78 *Now let it work . . . wilt* – "Now let
my words have their effect (*work*).
Destruction (*Mischief*) has begun.
Let it go on now as it pleases".

1 PLEBEIAN

Never, never! Come, away, away!
We 'll burn his body in the holy place,[76]
And with the brands fire the traitors' houses.[77]
Take up the body.   250

2 PLEBEIAN

Go, fetch fire!

3 PLEBEIAN

Pluck down benches!

4 PLEBEIAN

Pluck down forms, windows, anything!

[*Exeunt* Plebeians *with the body*

ANTONY

Now let it work! Mischief, thou art afoot,
Take thou what course thou wilt![78]

Enter a Servant

How now, fellow?   255

SERVANT

Sir, Octavius is already come to Rome.

ANTONY

Where is he?

SERVANT

He and Lepidus are at Caesar's house.

159

79 *upon a wish. Fortune is merry* –
"at the very moment I want. The
goddess of fortune is laughing . . ."

80 *Belike they had some notice* – "Perhaps they were told . . ."

1 After the tragedy of the last scene there is some opportunity for laughter
here – but the humour is cruel. Cinna, the poet, is killed by the crowd 'for
his bad verses'. The scene shows the foolishness of the mob.

2 *And things unluckily . . . fantasy* –
"and things which are signs of
disaster (*unluckily*) burden (*charge*)
my imagination (*fantasy*)".

3 *I have no will . . . leads me forth* –
"I have no wish to go wandering
outside, yet something seems to
force me to come out".

ANTONY

And thither will I straight, to visit him:
He comes upon a wish. Fortune is merry,[79]   260
And in this mood will give us any thing.

SERVANT

I heard him say, Brutus and Cassius
Are rid like madmen through the gates of Rome.

ANTONY

Belike they had some notice[80] of the people,
How I had moved them. Bring me to Octavius.   265

[*Exeunt*

Scene III. A street.[1]
Enter CINNA *the* poet.

CINNA

I dreamt tonight that I did feast with Caesar,
And things unluckily charge my fantasy;[2]
I have no will to wander forth of doors,
Yet something leads me forth.[3]

Enter Plebeians

1 PLEBEIAN

What is your name?   5

2 PLEBEIAN

Whither are you going?

3 PLEBEIAN

Where do you dwell?

4 PLEBEIAN

Are you a married man, or a bachelor?

4 *directly* – "at once", also "clearly".
5 *you were best* – "or it will be the worse for you".
6 *bear me a bang* – "get a knock from me".
7 *proceed directly* – "go on at once".

8 *Directly, I am going* – "I am going, by the quickest way . . ."
9 *That matter is answered directly* – "That question (*matter*) is clearly (*directly*) answered".

2 PLEBEIAN

Answer every man directly.[4]

1 PLEBEIAN

Ay, and briefly.   10

4 PLEBEIAN

Ay, and wisely.

3 PLEBEIAN

Ay, and truly, you were best.[5]

CINNA

What is my name? Whither am I going? Where do I dwell?
Am I a married man, or a bachelor? Then to answer every man,
directly and briefly, wisely and truly: wisely I say, I am a   15
bachelor.

2 PLEBEIAN

That 's as much as to say they are fools that marry; you 'll
bear me a bang[6] for that, I fear; proceed directly.[7]

CINNA

Directly, I am going[8] to Caesar's funeral.

1 PLEBEIAN

As a friend, or an enemy?   20

CINNA

As a friend.

2 PLEBEIAN

That matter is answered directly.[9]

4 PLEBEIAN

For your dwelling: briefly.

10 *his bad verses* – "the poor quality of his poetry".

11 *pluck but his name . . . going* – "only pull his name out of his heart, and then let him go".

CINNA

Briefly, I dwell by the Capitol.

3 PLEBEIAN

Your name, sir, truly.   25

CINNA

Truly, my name is Cinna.

1 PLEBEIAN

Tear him to pieces; he 's a conspirator.

CINNA

I am Cinna the poet, I am Cinna the poet!

4 PLEBEIAN

Tear him for his bad verses,[10] tear him for his bad verses.

CINNA

I am not Cinna the conspirator.   30

4 PLEBEIAN

It is no matter; his name 's Cinna; pluck but his name out of
his heart, and turn him going.[11]

3 PLEBEIAN

Tear him, tear him! Come, brands, ho, fire-brands! To
Brutus', to Cassius', burn all! Some to Decius' house, and
some to Casca's; some to Ligarius'! Away, go!   35

[*Exeunt all the* Plebeians

1 Antony, Octavius and Lepidus, the three men of power (known together as the triumvirate) are marking on their lists which men are to die as enemies of Caesar and of the triumvirate. Lepidus is sent to fetch the will: Antony intends not to give the people what Caesar wished them to have. He explains to Octavius that Lepidus shall be their tool as long as it suits them; afterwards they will take away his power. Now they must gather their forces to defeat Brutus and Cassius.

2 *are pricked* – "we have marked on the list" (*pricked*, 'marked with a dot or by actually pricking a little hole into the paper').

3 *Prick him down* – "Mark him for death".

4 *damn* – "condemn".

5 *determine ... charge* – "decide how to save some of the expense".

for we are at the stake,[19]
And bayed about with many enemies

166

ACT FOUR

Scene I. A house in Rome.[1]
ANTONY, OCTAVIUS, *and* LEPIDUS, *seated at a table.*

ANTONY

These many then shall die; their names are pricked.[2]

OCTAVIUS

Your brother too must die. Consent you, Lepidus?

LEPIDUS

I do consent –

OCTAVIUS

           Prick him down,[3] Antony.   5

LEPIDUS

Upon condition Publius shall not live,
Who is your sister's son, Mark Antony.

ANTONY

He shall not live; look, with a spot I damn[4] him.
But Lepidus, go you to Caesar's house:
Fetch the will hither, and we shall determine
How to cut off some charge[5] in legacies.

LEPIDUS

What? Shall I find you here?   10

OCTAVIUS

Or here, or at the Capitol.

                      [*Exit* LEPIDUS

167

6 *unmeritable* – "undeserving, who deserves no consideration".

7 *Is it fit . . . share it?* – "Is it right (*fit*) that, when the world, in its three parts (*threefold* – Europe, Asia and Africa), is divided between us, he should be accepted as (*stand*) one of the three rulers to have a share?"

8 *So you thought him . . . proscription* – "You had this opinion of him and yet let him have a vote (*voice*) on which men should be marked for death in our sad and cruel judgement (*black sentence*) and sentence of death (*proscription*)".

9 *I have seen more days . . . loads* – "I am older and more experienced than you, and, although we load Lepidus with honours so as to keep ourselves free of various hateful things that could be said of us by spiteful enemies . . ." (Lepidus is to do the 'dirty work'.)

10 *He shall but bear them . . . business* – "he shall have and carry these honours only as a donkey carries a load of treasure, groaning and sweating with the hard work (*business*)".

11 *And having brought our treasure . . . commons* – "And when he has carried our gold where we wish (*will*), then we take the load off (*down*), and let him loose (*turn him off*), like a donkey free of his load (*empty*), to look like a fool (*to shake his ears*) and pick up what grass he can find (*graze*) on the common land like all the others (*in commons*)". (Lepidus shall have honour and responsibility as long as it suits them. When his work is done they will take away his power.)

12 *tried* – "experienced".

13 *I do appoint . . . provender* – "I allow (*appoint*) him a good amount (*store*) of food".

14 *To wind, to stop . . . but so* – "to turn (*wind*), to stop, to gallop straight (*directly*) on, the movement of his body (*His corporal motion*) controlled by my wishes (*spirit*), and in some ways (*taste*), Lepidus is nothing more (*but so*)".

ANTONY

This is a slight, unmeritable⁶ man,
Meet to be sent on errands. Is it fit,
The three-fold world divided, he should stand
One of the three to share it?⁷

OCTAVIUS

        So you thought him,   15
And took his voice who should be pricked to die
In our black sentence and proscription. ⁸

ANTONY

Octavius, I have seen more days than you,
And though we lay these honours on this man,
To ease ourselves of divers slanderous loads,⁹   20
He shall but bear them as the ass bears gold,
To groan and sweat under the business,¹⁰
Either led or driven, as we point the way;
And having brought our treasure where we will,
Then take we down his load, and turn him off   25
Like to the empty ass, to shake his ears,
And graze in commons.¹¹

OCTAVIUS

        You may do your will;
But he's a tried¹² and valiant soldier.

ANTONY

So is my horse, Octavius, and, for that,
I do appoint him store of provender.¹³   30
It is a creature that I teach to fight,
To wind, to stop, to run directly on,
His corporal motion governed by my spirit,
And in some taste is Lepidus but so;¹⁴
He must be taught, and trained, and bid go forth;   35

169

15 *A barren-spirited fellow . . . Begin his fashion* – "a man who has no ideas (*barren-spirited*), who delights in aiming at (*object*, 'thing aimed at'), having theories (*arts*) about, and copying, those things (*imitations*) which other men have given up and found stale long ago, but which he thinks the newest fashion". [The word *orts*, 'scraps, fragments', is sometimes given instead of *arts*; the meaning is then "getting scraps of" instead of "having theories about".]

16 *But as a property* – "except as a tool".

17 *Listen great things . . . be combined* – "Listen to important news. Brutus and Cassius are calling up men into their army; we must at once advance against them (*straight make head*); and so let our forces be joined together".

18 *Our best friends made . . . surest answeréd* – "let us get the support of our best friends and use all our efforts (*means stretched*) and decide quickly (*presently go sit in council*) the best way to make public (*disclose*) the news which people do not yet know (*covert matters*), and the safest (*surest*) way to meet (*answer*) those dangers which are known to everybody (*open*)".

19 *for we are at the stake . . . many enemies* – "for we are like captured bears tied up to a post (*stake*), and barked at by (*bayed about with*) the dogs attacking them".

20 *Millions of mischief* – "any number of evil things which they would like to do against us".

1 Brutus and Cassius, with their armies, meet to join forces. There is already a coolness between them.

2 *Stand, ho!* – "Halt, there!"

3 *is come To do you salutation* – "has come to bring you greetings".

A barren-spirited fellow; one that feeds
On objects, arts, and imitations,
Which, out of use and staled by other men,
Begin his fashion.[15] Do not talk of him
But as a property.[16] And now, Octavius,   40
Listen great things. Brutus and Cassius
Are levying powers; we must straight make head;
Therefore let our alliance be combined,[17]
Our best friends made, our means stretched,
And let us presently go sit in council   45
How covert matters may be best disclosed,
And open perils surest answeréd.[18]

OCTAVIUS

Let us do so; for we are at the stake,
And bayed about with many enemies,[19]
And some that smile have in their hearts, I fear,   50
Millions of mischief.[20]

                                                [Exeunt

Scene II. Camp near Sardis. In front of Brutus' tent.[1]
Drum. Enter BRUTUS, LUCILIUS, *and* Soldiers.
TITINIUS *and* PINDARUS *meet them.*

BRUTUS

Stand, ho![2]

LUCILIUS

Give the word, ho, and stand!

BRUTUS

What now, Lucilius? Is Cassius near?

LUCILIUS

He is at hand, and Pindarus is come
To do you salutation[3] from his master.   5

4 *He greets me well . . . shall be satisfied* – "I have no complaint about the way he greets me. This is my complaint about your master: because of some change in himself or through the bad conduct of some of his officers (*by ill officers*) he has given me good reason (*worthy cause*) to be displeased with some things that have happened. But, if he is near at hand, we can discuss it and he can explain." [The phrase *In his own change* is sometimes given as *In his own charge*, meaning "through his own orders".]

5 *will appear Such as he is . . . and honour* – "will show himself as he is, a man full of wisdom and just deeds" (*full of regard* can mean 'able to look carefully at all circumstances'; also 'worthy of being well thought of by others').

6 *He is not doubted . . . be resolved* – "We do not doubt that he is a man of honour. Let me have a word with you, Lucilius, about his manner to you; tell me about it".

7 *But not with such familiar instances . . . used of old* – "But not with such little details of friendship (*familiar instances*), nor with such open (*free*) and friendly talk (*conference*) as he used to (*hath used*) in the past (*of old*)".

8 *A hot friend cooling* – "a very close friend now becoming unfriendly".

9 *Ever note . . . love* "Always notice, Lucilius, when true friendship . . ."

10 *It useth . . . simple faith* – "it makes use of too much pretended (*enforcéd*) politeness (*ceremony*). There is nothing false (*no tricks*) in the open (*plain*) and true loyalty (*simple faith*) of a friend".

11 *But hollow men . . . Sink in the trial* – "but men who are false (*hollow*) inside, like horses who are eager to enter battle (*hot*) as long as they are held back (*at hand*), make a fine show of courage (*gallant show*) and seem as if they will be full of spirit (*make promise of their mettle*); but when the time comes for them to gallop hard, spurred on by their riders (*when they should endure the bloody spur*), they let their heads, decorated with plumes of feathers, sink down (*fall their crests*) and like worthless horses (*jades*) which cannot be relied on (*deceitful*) fail (*sink*) in the test (*trial*)".

172

BRUTUS

He greets me well. Your master, Pindarus,
In his own change, or by ill officers,
Hath given me some worthy cause to wish
Things done, undone. But if he be at hand
I shall be satisfied.[4]

PINDARUS

          I do not doubt   10
But that my noble master will appear
Such as he is, full of regard, and honour.[5]

BRUTUS

He is not doubted. A word, Lucilius,
How he received you; let me be resolved.[6]

LUCILIUS

With courtesy, and with respect enough,   15
But not with such familiar instances,
Nor with such free and friendly conference
As he hath used of old.[7]

BRUTUS

          Thou hast described
A hot friend cooling.[8] Ever note, Lucilius,
When love[9] begins to sicken and decay   20
It useth an enforcéd ceremony.
There are no tricks in plain and simple faith;[10]
But hollow men, like horses hot at hand,
Make gallant show and promise of their mettle;
But when they should endure the bloody spur,   25
They fall their crests, and like deceitful jades
Sink in the trial.[11] Comes his army on?

12 *They mean . . . quartered* – "They intend to have lodgings tonight in Sardis".

13 *the horse in general* – "most of the horse-soldiers".

14 *you have done me wrong* – "you have behaved unfairly to me".

LUCILIUS

They mean this night in Sardis to be quartered;[12]
The greater part, the horse in general,[13]
Are come with Cassius.   30

[*Low march within*

BRUTUS

Hark, he is arrived;
March gently on to meet him.

Enter CASSIUS *and his* Powers

CASSIUS

Stand, ho!

BRUTUS

Stand, ho, speak the word along!

I SOLDIER

Stand.   35

2 SOLDIER

Stand.

3 SOLDIER

Stand.

CASSIUS

Most noble brother, you have done me wrong.[14]

BRUTUS

Judge me, you gods; wrong I mine enemies?
And if not so, how should I wrong a brother?   40

15 *this sober form . . . do them* – "you seem calm and fair-minded (*sober*) but underneath you have been very unjust, and when you are—"

16 *be content . . . softly* – "I would ask you, tell me quietly what you are complaining about".

17 *Which should perceive . . . us* – "who ought to see between us only firm friendship"

18 *enlarge your griefs . . . audience* – "tell me at length of your complaints and I will listen to you".

19 *lead their charges off* – "lead away the men under their orders".

20 *do you the like* – "you do the same".

21 *done our conference* – "finished our talk".

1 Cassius complains that Brutus has punished one of his supporters for taking bribes; Brutus accuses Cassius of selling official positions. Cassius claims to be a soldier of more experience, and Brutus, in return, accuses Cassius of refusing him money when he needed it. Cassius cries out in grief that Brutus loved Caesar more than he loves him. They become good friends again; Brutus tells Cassius that Portia is dead. They argue as to where the battle shall be fought, Brutus insisting that they march to Philippi, and Cassius unwillingly agrees. The ghost of Caesar appears to Brutus: it tells Brutus that Brutus will see him again at Philippi.

2 *doth appear . . . Lucius Pella* – "can be seen in this: You have found guilty (*condemned*) Lucius Pella and have punished him by public disgrace (*noted*) . . ."

3 *Wherein my letters . . . slighted off* – "and in this case you paid no attention at all to (*slighted off*) my letters, asking that he should be excused punishment as a friend of mine"

176

CASSIUS

Brutus, this sober form of yours hides wrongs,
And when you do them –[15]

BRUTUS

           Cassius, be content,
Speak your griefs softly;[16] I do know you well.
Before the eyes of both our armies here,
Which should perceive nothing but love from us,[17]   45
Let us not wrangle. Bid them move away;
Then in my tent, Cassius, enlarge your griefs,
And I will give you audience.[18]

CASSIUS

           Pindarus,
Bid our commanders lead their charges off[19]
A little from this ground.   50

BRUTUS

Lucilius, do you the like,[20] and let no man
Come to our tent till we have done our conference.[21]
Let Lucius and Titinius guard our door.

                             [*Exeunt*

Scene III. Brutus' tent.[1]
Enter BRUTUS *and* CASSIUS.

CASSIUS

That you have wronged me doth appear in this:
You have condemned and noted Lucius Pella[2]
For taking bribes here of the Sardians;
Wherein my letters, praying on his side,
Because I knew the man, were slighted off.[3]   5

177

4 *You wronged yourself* – "You put yourself in the wrong (you were yourself guilty)".

5 *That every nice offence ... comment* – "that every wrongdoing (*offence*) which an over-strict (*nice*) conscience would condemn, should be noticed and punished (*bear his comment*)".

6 *Are much condemned ... undeservers* – "are blamed by many as a man who likes to have his hand rubbed with gold, and who will market (*mart*) official positions, selling them to men who have no merit".

7 *You know ... else your last* – "You count on my old friendship for you when you say this; otherwise (*else*) I would certainly kill you".

8 *The name of Cassius ... head* – "Your name is a shield to (*honours*) this dishonesty (*corruption*) so that punishment (*chastisement*) does not show its face because of you (*therefore*)".

9 *What villain ... justice* – "What evil man among us stabbed Caesar unless he did so to bring justice to Rome?"

10 *But for supporting robbers* – "only because he allowed robbers to go unpunished".

BRUTUS

You wronged yourself[4] to write in such a case.

CASSIUS

In such a time as this it is not meet
That every nice offence should bear his comment.[5]

BRUTUS

Let me tell you, Cassius, you yourself
Are much condemned to have an itching palm,   10
To sell and mart your offices for gold
To undeservers.[6]

CASSIUS

I, an itching palm?
You know that you are Brutus that speaks this,
Or by the gods, this speech were else your last.[7]

BRUTUS

The name of Cassius honours this corruption,   15
And chastisement doth therefore hide his head.[8]

CASSIUS

Chastisement?

BRUTUS

Remember March, the Ides of March remember:
Did not great Julius bleed for justice' sake?
What villain touched his body, that did stab,   20
And not for justice?[9] What? Shall one of us,
That struck the foremost man of all this world,
But for supporting robbers,[10] shall we now,
Contaminate our fingers with base bribes
And sell the mighty space of our large honours   25

179

11 *the mighty space . . . graspéd thus* – "the great power of our important positions as leaders of Rome for a handful of worthless money".

12 *bay* – "bark at (in useless stupidity)".

13 *bait not me* – "Do not try to make me angry".

14 *you forget yourself . . . make conditions* – "You forget who you are when you try to tie me down with your rules (*hedge me in*). I am a soldier of more experience (*Older in practice*) and more able than you to decide what shall be done (*To make conditions*)".

15 *Go to* – "That's not true; you should be ashamed of yourself".

16 *Urge me no more* – "Do not drive me any further".

17 *Have mind upon your health* – "Think of your own safety".

18 *Must I give way . . . stares?* – "Am I to submit (*give way*) to your fierce temper (*rash choler*) and give you freedom (*room*) to say all you want? Am I to be afraid of the wild looks of a madman?"

180

For so much trash as may be graspéd thus ?[11]
I had rather be a dog, and bay[12] the moon,
Than such a Roman.

CASSIUS

        Brutus, bait not me,[13]
I 'll not endure it: you forget yourself
To hedge me in. I am a soldier, I,   30
Older in practice, abler than yourself
To make conditions.[14]

BRUTUS

        Go to;[15] you are not, Cassius.

CASSIUS

I am.

BRUTUS

I say you are not.

CASSIUS

Urge me no more;[16] I shall forget myself;   35
Have mind upon your health.[17] Tempt me no farther.

BRUTUS

Away, slight man!

CASSIUS

Is 't possible?

BRUTUS

        Hear me, for I will speak.
Must I give way and room to your rash choler?
Shall I be frighted when a madman stares?[18]   40

19 *Ay more: fret* - "Yes and more:
suffer the pain of anger ..."
20 *choleric* - "hot-tempered".
21 *budge* - "go back a single step".
22 *observe* - "watch and try to please".
23 *Must I stand . . . testy humour* -
"Must I stop what I am doing
(*stand*) and bend low, trying to
find shelter (*crouch*), because you
are in an irritable (*testy*) mood
(*humour*)?"
24 *You shall digest . . . split you* -
"You shall yourself swallow
(*digest*) the poison (*venom*) of your
anger and bad-temper (*spleen*)
even if it kills you" (*split*, 'cut in
two').

25 *I'll use you . . . are waspish* - "I'll
make a habit of being amused by
you, yes, even of laughing at you,
when you are stinging like a wasp
with your bitter words".
26 *Let it appear so* - "Show me how".
27 *vaunting* - "boasting".
28 *I shall be glad to learn of noble men* -
"I shall be pleased to learn how to
be a soldier from such a noble
man as you are".
29 *When Caesar lived . . . moved me* -
"When Caesar was alive, even he
would not have dared to arouse
my anger in this way".

CASSIUS

O ye gods, ye gods, must I endure all this?

BRUTUS

All this? Ay more: fret[19] till your proud heart break.
Go show your slaves how choleric[20] you are,
And make your bondmen tremble. Must I budge?[21]
Must I observe[22] you? Must I stand and crouch   45
Under your testy humour?[23] By the gods,
You shall digest the venom of your spleen
Though it do split you.[24] For, from this day forth,
I 'll use you for my mirth, yea for my laughter,
When you are waspish.[25]

CASSIUS

Is it come to this?   50

BRUTUS

You say, you are a better soldier:
Let it appear so;[26] make your vaunting[27] true,
And it shall please me well. For mine own part,
I shall be glad to learn of noble men.[28]

CASSIUS

You wrong me every way; you wrong me, Brutus: 55
I said, an elder soldier, not a better.
Did I say better?

BRUTUS

If you did, I care not.

CASSIUS

When Caesar lived, he durst not thus have moved me.[29]

183

30 *tempted him* – "tried his temper".
31 *presume too much upon my love* – "rely too much upon my friend-ship for you".
32 *There is no terror . . . respect not* – "There is nothing to frighten me (*no terror*) in your threats, for my honour (*honesty*) is like such strong armour that your words blow past me like the empty (*idle*) wind, for which I care nothing (*respect not*)".
33 *denied* – "refused"

34 *For I can raise . . . means* – "I asked you for the money because I cannot get money together myself by any evil methods".
35 *I had rather coin . . . indirection* – "I would rather turn my heart into gold and let the drops of my blood be used as coins (*drachmas*, 'silver coins') than squeeze (*wring*) from the hardworking (*hard*) hands of country labourers their little bits of worthless money (*vile trash*) by any dishonesty (*indirection*)".
36 *legions* – "forces".

BRUTUS

Peace, peace! You durst not so have tempted him.[30]

CASSIUS

I durst not?   60

BRUTUS

No.

CASSIUS

What? Durst not tempt him?

BRUTUS

                    For your life you durst not.

CASSIUS

Do not presume too much upon my love,[31]
I may do that I shall be sorry for.

BRUTUS

You have done that you should be sorry for.   65
There is no terror, Cassius, in your threats:
For I am armed so strong in honesty
That they pass by me as the idle wind
Which I respect not.[32] I did send to you
For certain sums of gold, which you denied[33] me,   70
For I can raise no money by vile means:[34]
By heaven, I had rather coin my heart,
And drop my blood for drachmas, than to wring
From the hard hands of peasants their vile trash
By any indirection.[35] I did send   75
To you for gold to pay my legions,[36]
Which you denied me; was that done like Cassius?
Should I have answered Caius Cassius so?
When Marcus Brutus grows so covetous,

37 *To lock such rascal counters* – "that he locks up such wicked bits of money".

38 *He was but a fool . . . infirmities* – "It was only that the messenger was a fool. Brutus has broken (*rived*) my heart. A true friend ought to accept (*should bear*) and not criticise those faults (*infirmities*) which his friend cannot help . . ."

39 *practise them on me* – "use them against me so as to trick me" (*practise* has two meanings – 'use', 'trick').

40 *Olympus*, high mountain, home of the gods in Greece.

41 *alone on Cassius* – "on Cassius only".

To lock such rascal counters[37] from his friends,   80
Be ready, gods, with all your thunder-bolts;
Dash him to pieces!

CASSIUS

I denied you not.

BRUTUS

You did.

CASSIUS

I did not. He was but a fool
That brought my answer back. Brutus hath rived my heart.
A friend should bear his friend's infirmities,[38]   85
But Brutus makes mine greater than they are.

BRUTUS

I do not, till you practise them on me.[39]

CASSIUS

You love me not.

BRUTUS

I do not like your faults.

CASSIUS

A friendly eye could never see such faults.

BRUTUS

A flatterer's would not, though they do appear   90
As huge as high Olympus.[40]

CASSIUS

Come, Antony, and young Octavius, come,
Revenge yourselves alone on Cassius,[41]

187

42 *braved by his brother . . . mine eyes –*
"dared to do his worst (*braved*)
by one he thought his brother,
scolded (*checked*) like a slave (*bond-man*), all his mistakes noticed,
written down in a notebook,
repeated and learned by heart
(*conned by rote*) to throw into my
face. I could die of grief".

43 *Dearer than Pluto's mine –* "more
valuable than even the goldmine
of Plutus" (*Plutus*, god of riches,
and *Pluto*, god of the underworld,
were often spoken of by Eliza-
bethan writers as if they were the
same).

44 *Be angry . . . scope –* "Lose your
temper whenever you please; you
shall have freedom (*scope*) to say
what you like".

45 *dishonour shall be humour –* "your
insults (*dishonour*) shall not be
taken seriously; they shall be
looked on as coming from a mood
(*humour*) of anger".

46 *yokéd –* "joined in a piece of work
(as two oxen are joined together)".

47 *That carries anger . . . is cold again –*
"That keeps his anger inside as a
flint (sharp stone) keeps its spark,
and when it is struck again and
again (*much enforcéd*) gives off a
quick spark and then is cold again
at once". So Brutus claims that,
when made angry by Cassius, he
has lost his temper only for a
second.

48 *Hath Cassius lived . . . vexeth
him? –* "Have I lived so long that
I am now only something for my
dear Brutus to mock and laugh
at, when I am (or when Brutus is)
upset by worry (*grief*) and ill
humour (*blood ill tempered*) ?"

For Cassius is aweary of the world,
Hated by one he loves, braved by his brother,   95
Checked like a bondman, all his faults observed,
Set in a note-book, learned, and conned by rote
To cast into my teeth. O, I could weep
My spirit from mine eyes.[42] There is my dagger,
And here my naked breast: within, a heart   100
Dearer than Pluto's mine,[43] richer than gold:
If that thou beest a Roman, take it forth.
I, that denied thee gold, will give my heart:
Strike as thou didst at Caesar. For I know,
When thou didst hate him worst, thou lovedst him better   105
Than ever thou lovedst Cassius.

BRUTUS

                    Sheathe your dagger.
Be angry when you will, it shall have scope:[44]
Do what you will, dishonour shall be humour.[45]
O Cassius, you are yokéd[46] with a lamb
That carries anger as the flint bears fire,   110
Who, much enforcéd, shows a hasty spark,
And straight is cold again.[47]

CASSIUS

                    Hath Cassius lived
To be but mirth and laughter to his Brutus,
When grief and blood ill tempered vexeth him?[48]

BRUTUS

When I spoke that, I was ill tempered too.   115

CASSIUS

Do you confess so much? Give me your hand.

BRUTUS

And my heart too.

189

49 *What's the matter?* – "What is wrong? Why are you so upset?"

50 *bear with me . . . Makes me forgetful* – "put up with me (*bear with me*) when that habit of sudden anger (*rash humour*) which I got from my mother makes me forget how to behave".

51 *When you are over-earnest . . . and leave you so* – "when you are too serious (*over-earnest*) with your friend Brutus, he will think it is your mother speaking angrily, and go away while you cool down".

52 *stay* – "stop".

53 *What's the matter?* – "Why is there this disturbance?"

CASSIUS

O Brutus!

BRUTUS

What 's the matter?⁴⁹

CASSIUS

Have not you love enough to bear with me,
When that rash humour which my mother gave me
Makes me forgetful?⁵⁰

BRUTUS

Yes, Cassius, and from henceforth   120
When you are over-earnest with your Brutus,
He 'll think your mother chides, and leave you so.⁵¹

POET

[*Within*] Let me go in to see the generals.
There is some grudge between them; 't is not meet
They be alone.

LUCILIUS

[*Within*] You shall not come to them.   125

POET

[*Within*] Nothing but death shall stay⁵² me.

Enter POET, *followed by* LUCILIUS, TITINIUS *and* LUCIUS

CASSIUS

How now? What 's the matter?⁵³

191

54 *how vilely doth this cynic rhyme!* –
"what bad verse this dog (*cynic*)
makes!"

55 *sirrah: saucy fellow* – "fellow; disrespectful creature".

56 *Bear with him . . . fashion* – "Do
not be angry, Brutus; he is always
like this".

57 *I 'll know his humour . . . Companion, hence* – "I will make allow-
ances for (*know*) what he is like
(*his humour*), if he agrees that not
every time is the right time for
jesting. What good are these
dancing (*jigging*) fools in time of
war? Clown, take yourself off!"

POET

For shame, you generals; what do you mean?
Love, and be friends, as two such men should be,
For I have seen more years, I 'm sure, than ye.   130

CASSIUS

Ha, ha, how vilely doth this cynic rhyme![54]

BRUTUS

Get you hence, sirrah: saucy fellow,[55] hence.

CASSIUS

Bear with him Brutus, 't is his fashion.[56]

BRUTUS

I 'll know his humour when he knows his time.
What should the wars do with these jigging fools?   135
Companion, hence![57]

CASSIUS

Away, away be gone.

[Exit POET

BRUTUS

Lucilius and Titinius, bid the commanders
Prepare to lodge their companies tonight.

CASSIUS

And come yourselves, and bring Messala with you
Immediately to us.

[Exeunt LUCILIUS and TITINIUS

58 *sick of many griefs* – "wearied with many sorrows".

59 *Of your philosophy . . . accidental evils* – "If you let yourself be troubled by (*give place to*) things that happen by chance (*accidental evils*), then you forget (*make no use of*) your Stoic philosophy". (Those who followed the Stoic system of thought believed in calm endurance of all hardship.)

60 *How 'scaped I killing . . . sickness?* – "How did I escape death at your hands when I made you so angry? A grief (*loss*) that touches you so close (*touching*) is not to be endured (*insupportable*). What was the cause of her death?"

61 *Impatient of my absence, And grief* – "She could not endure my being away and was full of sorrow . . ."

62 *with her death That tidings came* – "I heard the news (*tidings*) of how strong their forces were at the same time as I heard the news of her death".

63 *With this she fell distract . . . swallowed fire* – "Because of this she became mad and, when her servants were not there, choked herself with hot coals from the fire".

BRUTUS
Lucius, a bowl of wine.   140

[*Exit* LUCIUS

CASSIUS
I did not think you could have been so angry.

BRUTUS
O Cassius, I am sick of many griefs.[58]

CASSIUS
Of your philosophy you make no use,
If you give place to accidental evils.[59]

BRUTUS
No man bears sorrow better. Portia is dead!   145

CASSIUS
Ha? Portia?

BRUTUS
She is dead.

CASSIUS
How 'scaped I killing when I crossed you so?
O insupportable and touching loss!
Upon what sickness?[60]

BRUTUS
                    Impatient of my absence,   150
And grief,[61] that young Octavius with Mark Antony
Have made themselves so strong; for with her death
That tidings came.[62] With this she fell distract
And, her attendants absent, swallowed fire.[63]

64 *I bury all unkindness* – "I put an end to all our quarrelling".

65 *o'er-swell* – "run over".

66 *call in question our necessities* – "discuss what we must do".

Give me a bowl of wine

CASSIUS

And died so?

BRUTUS

Even so.

CASSIUS

O ye immortal gods!   155

Re-enter LUCIUS *with wine, and tapers*

BRUTUS

Speak no more of her. Give me a bowl of wine;
In this I bury all unkindness,[64] Cassius.

[*Drinks*

CASSIUS

My heart is thirsty for that noble pledge.
Fill, Lucius, till the wine o'er-swell[65] the cup;
I cannot drink too much of Brutus' love.   160

[*Drinks*
[*Exit* LUCIUS

Re-enter TITINIUS *and* MESSALA

BRUTUS

Come in, Titinius! Welcome, good Messala.
Now sit we close about this taper here,
And call in question our necessities.[66]

CASSIUS

Portia, art thou gone?

197

67 *Come down upon us . . . expedition* –
"are coming to attack us with a
great army, advancing in haste
(*expedition*) . . ."
68 *proscription, and bills of outlawry* –
"including their names on the list
of those to die and declaring them
enemies of the state . . ."
69 *Therein* – "On this point".

70 *Had you your letters . . . my lord?*
It is possible that this conversation,
in which Brutus seems to hear the
news of Portia's death for the
first time from Messala, is part of
an earlier draft and should have
been taken out of the finished
play.

BRUTUS

        No more, I pray you.
Messala, I have here receivéd letters,   165
That young Octavius and Mark Antony
Come down upon us with a mighty power,
Bending their expedition[67] toward Philippi.

MESSALA

Myself have letters of the self-same tenor.

BRUTUS

With what addition?   170

MESSALA

That by proscription, and bills of outlawry,[68]
Octavius, Antony, and Lepidus,
Have put to death an hundred senators.

BRUTUS

Therein[69] our letters do not well agree:
Mine speak of seventy senators that died   175
By their proscriptions, Cicero being one.

CASSIUS

Cicero one?

MESSALA

        Cicero is dead,
And by that order of proscription.
Had you your letters from your wife, my lord?[70]

BRUTUS

No, Messala.   180

MESSALA

Nor nothing in your letters writ of her?

71 *We must die, Messala . . . must die once* – "Death is natural for all of us. Through thinking that Portia will have to die at some time . . ."

72 *as much of this in art as you* – "as much patience as you in theory (art)".

73 *to our work alive* – "let us get back to the business of living!"

BRUTUS

Nothing, Messala.

MESSALA

That, methinks, is strange.

BRUTUS

Why ask you? Hear you aught of her in yours?

MESSALA

No, my lord.

BRUTUS

Now, as you are a Roman, tell me true.   185

MESSALA

Then, like a Roman, bear the truth I tell,
For certain she is dead, and by strange manner.

BRUTUS

Why, farewell, Portia. We must die, Messala.
With meditating that she must die once,[71]
I have the patience to endure it now.   190

MESSALA

Even so great men great losses should endure.

CASSIUS   C

I have as much of this in art as you,[72]
But yet my nature could not bear it so.

BRUTUS

Well, to our work alive![73] What do you think
Of marching to Philippi presently?   195

74 *waste his means* – "wear out what he has".

75 *Doing himself offence . . . and nimble-ness* – "harming himself, while we, staying in our positions (*lying still*), do not get tired and can move about quickly when we have to defend ourselves".

76 *Good reasons . . . grudged us contribution* – "Good arguments (*reasons*) must of necessity (*force*) be over-come by better ones. The people between ('*twixt*) Philippi and this place (*ground*) only (*but*) seem to support us (*stand in affection*), because they are compelled (*forced*) to: for they have been unwilling to give (*grudged*) us men and stores".

77 *The enemy . . . new added* – "If Antony and Octavius march through their lands, they will increase their number of soldiers, and will advance against us having been given food (*refreshed*), and extra forces (*new added*) . . ."

78 *From which advantage . . . at our back* – "We shall prevent the enemy getting these advantages if we fight against him at Philippi, after *we* have marched through this country (*These people at our back*)".

79 *Under your pardon . . . cause is ripe* – "Forgive me, but I must go on. You must take into account also that we have called for support from all our friends and we can get no more help. Our regiments (*legions*) are as full as we shall get them (*brim-full*, 'full to over-flowing'); this is the moment to fight for our beliefs (*cause*)".

CASSIUS

I do not think it good.

BRUTUS

Your reason?

CASSIUS

This it is:
'T is better that the enemy seek us;
So shall he waste his means,[74] weary his soldiers,
Doing himself offence, whilst we lying still,
Are full of rest, defence, and nimbleness.[75]   200

BRUTUS

Good reasons must of force give place to better.
The people 'twixt Philippi and this ground
Do stand but in a forced affection:
For they have grudged us contribution.[76]
The enemy, marching along by them,   205
By them shall make a fuller number up,
Come on refreshed, new added,[77] and encouraged;
From which advantage shall we cut him off,
If at Philippi we do face him there,
These people at our back.[78]

CASSIUS

Hear me, good brother.   210

BRUTUS

Under your pardon. You must note beside
That we have tried the utmost of our friends,
Our legions are brim-full, our cause is ripe;[79]
The enemy increaseth every day;
We, at the height, are ready to decline.   215
There is a tide in the affairs of men,

80 *There is a tide ... and in miseries* –
"Just as there is a tide in the sea
so there is a tide in the plans and
doings (*affairs*) of men. If the
opportunity is taken at its height
(*flood*, 'high tide'), good fortune
follows. If the chance is not taken
(*omitted*), all the rest of their life
is like travelling in a boat which
cannot get beyond shallow water
and ill luck".

81 *On such a full sea ... lose our ven-*
tures – "On such a high tide (*full*
sea) we are now floating, and we
must take advantage of (*take*) the
current while it is useful (*serves*),
or else lose the goods which we
are risking (*our ventures*), just as
all merchants and ship-owners
must".

82 *with your will* – "as you wish".

83 *The deep of night ... rest* – "While
we have been talking, the darkness
of night has stolen upon us, and,
as men, we must have the sleep we
need, but we will take only a little
rest, not a generous allowance"
(*niggard*, 'be ungenerous to').

84 *gown* – "dressing-gown".

Which, taken at the flood, leads on to fortune:
Omitted, all the voyage of their life,
Is bound in shallows and in miseries. [80]
On such a full sea are we now afloat,   220
And we must take the current when it serves,
Or lose our ventures. [81]

CASSIUS

Then, with your will, [82] go on:
We 'll along ourselves, and meet them at Philippi.

BRUTUS

The deep of night is crept upon our talk,   225
And nature must obey necessity,
Which we will niggard with a little rest. [83]
There is no more to say?

CASSIUS

                No more. Good night.
Early tomorrow will we rise, and hence.

Re-enter LUCIUS

BRUTUS

Lucius, my gown; [84] farewell, good Messala,   230

                                        [*Exit* LUCIUS

Good night, Titinius. Noble, noble Cassius,
Good night, and good repose.

CASSIUS

                O my dear brother,
This was an ill beginning of the night.
Never come such division 'tween our souls!
Let it not, Brutus.

85 *o'er-watched* – "tired with staying
awake too long".

BRUTUS

Everything is well.   235

CASSIUS

Good night, my lord.

BRUTUS

Good night, good brother.

TITINIUS: MESSALA

Good night, Lord Brutus.

BRUTUS

Farewell every one.

[*Exeunt* CASSIUS, TITINIUS *and* MESSALA

Re-enter LUCIUS *with the gown*

Give me the gown. Where is thy instrument?

LUCIUS

Here, in the tent.

BRUTUS

What, thou speakst drowsily?
Poor knave, I blame thee not; thou art o'er-watched. [85]   240
Call Claudius, and some other of my men;
I 'll have them sleep on cushions in my tent.

LUCIUS

Varro and Claudius!

Enter VARRO *and* CLAUDIUS

VARRO

Calls my lord?

86 *raise you . . . On business* – "ask you to get up later to take a message".

87 *So please you . . . your pleasure* – "If you wish, we will stay up and keep awake until you want us".

88 *otherwise bethink me* – "decide differently (not to send the message)".

89 *Bear with me . . . strain or two ?* – "Forgive me, please, my dear boy. I am very forgetful. Can you keep open your sleepy eyes for a time and play a tune or so on your instrument ?"

BRUTUS

I pray you, sirs, lie in my tent and sleep;   245
It may be I shall raise you by and by
On business[86] to my brother Cassius.

VARRO

So please you, we will stand, and watch your pleasure.[87]

BRUTUS

I will not have it so. Lie down, good sirs;
It may be I shall otherwise bethink me.[88]   250
Look, Lucius, here 's the book I sought for so;
I put it in the pocket of my gown.

[VARRO *and* CLAUDIUS *lie down*

LUCIUS

I was sure your lordship did not give it me.

BRUTUS

Bear with me, good boy; I am much forgetful.
Canst thou hold up thy heavy eyes awhile,   255
And touch thy instrument a strain or two?[89]

LUCIUS

Ay, my lord, an 't please you.

BRUTUS

                        It does, my boy:
I trouble thee too much, but thou art willing.

LUCIUS

It is my duty, sir.

209

90 *I should not urge . . . a time of rest* –
"I ought not to press (*urge*) you to
serve me more than you are able.
I know that young bodies need
(*look for*) sleep".

91 *It was well done* – "I am glad you
have done so".

92 *O murderous slumber . . . leaden
mace* – "O sleep, so like death, do
you lay your hammer of sleep,
heavy as lead . . ."

93 *knave* – "boy".

94 *If thou dost nod . . . thy instrument* –
"If your head falls forward, you
will break your instrument".

95 *it is the weakness . . . apparition* –
"I have something wrong with
my eyes that makes me see this
strange (*monstrous*) thing appearing".

96 *stare* – "stand on end".

BRUTUS

I should not urge thy duty past thy might,   260
I know young bloods look for a time of rest.[90]

LUCIUS

I have slept, my lord, already.

BRUTUS

It was well done,[91] and thou shalt sleep again;
I will not hold thee long. If I do live,
I will be good to thee.   265

[Music, and a song

This is a sleepy tune. O murderous slumber,
Layst thou thy leaden mace[92] upon my boy
That plays thee music? Gentle knave,[93] good night.
I will not do thee so much wrong to wake thee.
If thou dost nod, thou breakst thy instrument;[94]   270
I 'll take it from thee, and, good boy, good night.
Let me see, let me see; is not the leaf turned down
Where I left reading? Here it is, I think.

[Sits down

Enter the GHOST *of* CAESAR

How ill this taper burns. Ha! Who comes here?
I think it is the weakness of mine eyes   275
That shapes this monstrous apparition.[95]
It comes upon me. Art thou any thing?
Art thou some god, some angel, or some devil,
That makest my blood cold, and my hair to stare?[96]
Speak to me what thou art?   280

GHOST

Thy evil spirit, Brutus!

BRUTUS

Why comst thou?

211

97 *taken heart* – "found courage".   98 *false* – "not in tune".

GHOST

To tell thee thou shalt see me at Philippi.

BRUTUS

Well; then I shall see thee again?

GHOST

Ay, at Philippi.

BRUTUS

Why I will see thee at Philippi then.   285

[*Exit* GHOST

Now I have taken heart,[97] thou vanishest.
Ill spirit, I would hold more talk with thee.
Boy, Lucius! Varro! Claudius! Sirs, awake,
Claudius!

LUCIUS

The strings, my lord, are false.[98]

BRUTUS

He thinks he still is at his instrument.   290
Lucius, awake!

LUCIUS

My lord!

BRUTUS

Didst thou dream, Lucius, that thou so criedst out?

LUCIUS

My lord, I do not know that I did cry.

BRUTUS

Yes, that thou didst. Didst thou see any thing?   295

99 *commend me . . . before* – "give my
greetings to Cassius. Tell him to
let his army advance (*set on*) early
(*betimes*) in front of mine (*before*)".

LUCIUS

Nothing, my lord.

BRUTUS

Sleep again, Lucius. Sirrah, Claudius, fellow!
Thou! Awake!

VARRO

My lord?

CLAUDIUS

My lord?   300

BRUTUS

Why did you so cry out, sirs, in your sleep?

BOTH

Did we, my lord?

BRUTUS

Ay. Saw you any thing?

VARRO

No, my lord, I saw nothing.

CLAUDIUS

Nor I, my lord.   305

BRUTUS

Go, and commend me to my brother Cassius:
Bid him set on his powers betimes before,[99]
And we will follow.

BOTH

It shall be done, my lord.

[*Exeunt*

1 Octavius and Antony are arguing about the plan they have followed. They meet Brutus and Cassius for parley. Octavius intends to take revenge for Caesar's death and calls on Brutus and Cassius to bring their forces to battle. Cassius has some fear that the day may go badly for himself and Brutus.

2 *answered* – "fulfilled". (He speaks ironically, meaning the opposite of what he says. What they hoped has not happened.)

3 *keep* – "stay in".

4 *It proves not so . . . demand of them* – "It has not turned out like that; their forces (*battles*) are near (*at hand*). They intend to threaten (*warn*) us at Philippi here, coming to attack (*answering*) before we force them to do so (*do demand of them*)".

5 *Tut, I am in their bosoms . . . have courage* – "Don't worry about their advancing (*Tut*); I know what is in their hearts (*am in their bosoms*) and I know why they advance. They would be glad enough (*could be content*) to be in some other place, and they have come down from the hills with a courage (*bravery*) which is full of fear (*fearful*), hoping (*thinking*), by this appearance (*face*) of courage, to convince us (*fasten in our thoughts*) that they are brave".

6 *in gallant show* – "with splendid show, looking magnificent".

7 *bloody sign* – "red flag".

8 *something to be done* – "some action is about to be taken . . ."

9 *lead your battle softly on* – "lead your forces steadily on".

10 *even field* – "level ground".

ACT FIVE

Scene I. The plains of Philippi.[1]
Enter OCTAVIUS, ANTONY, *and their* Army.

OCTAVIUS

Now, Antony, our hopes are answered:[2]
You said the enemy would not come down,
But keep[3] the hills and upper regions;
It proves not so: their battles are at hand;
They mean to warn us at Philippi here,   5
Answering before we do demand of them.[4]

ANTONY

Tut, I am in their bosoms, and I know
Wherefore they do it. They could be content
To visit other places, and come down
With fearful bravery, thinking by this face   10
To fasten in our thoughts that they have courage;[5]
But 't is not so.

Enter a MESSENGER

MESSENGER

Prepare you, generals,
The enemy comes on in gallant show.[6]
Their bloody sign[7] of battle is hung out,   15
And something to be done[8] immediately.

ANTONY

Octavius, lead your battle softly on[9]
Upon the left hand of the even field.[10]

OCTAVIUS

Upon the right hand I; keep thou the left.

217

11 *Why do you cross me in this exigent?* –
"Why do you oppose (*cross*) me in
this moment of decision (*exigent*)?"

12 *but I will do so* – "but I intend to
take the right-hand side".

13 *They stand . . . parley* – "They have
stopped and wish to have some
discussion".

14 *Stand fast . . . out* – "Keep your
position, Titinius; we must come
out from the line of battle . . ."

15 *we will answer . . . some words* –
"we will attack when they do. Let
us go forward; the commanders
wish to speak to us".

16 *than bad strokes* – "than strokes made
on the list of names to show who
was sentenced to death (by Octavius, Antony and Lepidus)".

The plains of Philippi

ANTONY

Why do you cross me in this exigent?[11]   20

OCTAVIUS

I do not cross you: but I will do so.[12]

[*March*

Drum. Enter BRUTUS, CASSIUS, *and their* Army

BRUTUS

They stand, and would have parley.[13]

CASSIUS

Stand fast, Titinius; we must out[14] and talk.

OCTAVIUS

Mark Antony, shall we give sign of battle?

ANTONY

No, Caesar, we will answer on their charge.   25
Make forth; the generals would have some words.[15]

OCTAVIUS

Stir not until the signal.

BRUTUS

Words before blows? Is it so, countrymen?

OCTAVIUS

Not that we love words better, as you do.

BRUTUS

Good words are better than bad strokes,[16] Octavius.   30

17 *In your bad strokes* – "In *your* kind of bad strokes (when you stab to death)".

18 *Witness the hole* – "As we can see from the wound . . ."

19 *The posture of your blows . . . honey-less* – "How *you* can strike in battle we do not yet know; but as for your words, they have more honey than even the famous bees of Hybla – as we know from what happened at Caesar's funeral". Hybla, a district in Sicily, was famous for the honey produced there.

20 *Not stingless too* – "But my words could sting the crowds to take action".

21 *And very wisely threat before you sting* – "and you are sensible enough to threaten us before you attack us (since you know that we shall not be afraid of you afterwards)".

22 *when your vile daggers Hacked one another* – "when your wicked daggers struck one against the other".

23 *damnéd* – "who will be sent to ever-lasting punishment".

24 *This tongue had not offended . . . might have ruled* – "The tongue of Antony would not have insulted us today if my proposal (to kill Antony) had been accepted".

25 *the cause* – "the battle between us".

26 *The proof . . . redder drops* – "deciding the argument in battle (*the proof of it*) will make us shed drops of blood".

ANTONY

In your bad strokes,[17] Brutus, you give good words;
Witness the hole[18] you made in Caesar's heart,
Crying "Long live, hail Caesar!"

CASSIUS

                    Antony,
The posture of your blows are yet unknown;
But for your words, they rob the Hybla bees,   35
And leave them honeyless.[19]

ANTONY

                    Not stingless too.[20]

BRUTUS

O yes, and soundless too:
For you have stolen their buzzing, Antony,
And very wisely threat before you sting.[21]

ANTONY

Villains, you did not so, when your vile daggers   40
Hacked one another[22] in the sides of Caesar:
You showed your teeth like apes, and fawned like hounds,
And bowed like bondmen, kissing Caesar's feet;
Whilst damnéd[23] Casca, like a cur, behind
Struck Caesar on the neck. O you flatterers!   45

CASSIUS

Flatterers? Now, Brutus, thank yourself!
This tongue had not offended so today,
If Cassius might have ruled.[24]

OCTAVIUS

Come, come, the cause.[25] If arguing make us sweat,
The proof of it will turn to redder drops.[26]   50

221

27 *that the sword . . . again?* – "that I will sheathe the sword again?"

28 *or till another Caesar . . . of traitors* – "or until a second Caesar (Octavius Caesar) has been killed by the traitors (Brutus and Cassius)".

29 *strain* – "race".

30 *more honourable* – "with greater honour".

31 *worthless of such honour . . . a reveller* – "not worthy of so noble a death (as to die on Brutus' sword), in alliance with one who enjoys masques and entertainments". (A masque was a play, entertainment or dance in which those who took part would wear splendid and costly dress and have masks over their faces to hide who they were.)

32 *stomachs* – "the appetite or desire for fighting".

33 *blow wind . . . on the hazard* – "let the wind blow, the wave rise high and the ship toss. The storm has begun; we have risked everything and do not know what the result will be" (*hazard*, 'risk').

maskers and revellers[31]

Look! I draw a sword against conspirators.
When think you that the sword goes up again?[27]
Never till Caesar's three and thirty wounds
Be well avenged; or till another Caesar
Have added slaughter to the sword of traitors.[28]   55

BRUTUS

Caesar, thou canst not die by traitors' hands,
Unless thou bringst them with thee.

OCTAVIUS

So I hope.
I was not born to die on Brutus' sword.

BRUTUS

O if thou wert the noblest of thy strain,[29]   60
Young man, thou couldst not die more honourable.[30]

CASSIUS

A peevish schoolboy, worthless of such honour,
Joined with a masker and a reveller.[31]

ANTONY

Old Cassius still!

OCTAVIUS

                Come, Antony, away!
Defiance, traitors, hurl we in your teeth!   65
If you dare fight today, come to the field;
If not, when you have stomachs.[32]

                [*Exeunt* OCTAVIUS, ANTONY *and their* Army

CASSIUS

Why now, blow wind, swell billow, and swim bark:
The storm is up, and all is on the hazard.[33]

34 *Be thou my witness* – "you shall support what I say".

35 *As Pompey was.* Pompey hoped to wear down Caesar's strength and not to fight a battle against him; unfortunately for him he was mocked by his own captains and persuaded to fight by them; Caesar was then victorious in the battle of Pharsalia.

36 *am I compelled to set . . . our liberties* – "I am forced to risk (*set*) all our freedom on the result of one battle".

37 *that I held Epicurus strong, And his opinion* – "that I used to follow the teachings of Epicurus, and to believe in his opinion (that it is foolish to be superstitious)".

38 *And partly credit things that do presage* – "and have *some* belief in signs of bad luck".

39 *Coming from Sardis . . . fell* – "When we were marching from Sardis, two great eagles flew down (*fell*) on to our foremost standard (*our former ensign*)".

40 *Who to Philippi here consorted us* – "and they stayed with us until we reached Philippi here".

41 *steads* – "places".

42 *ravens, crows and kites*, all birds of prey which feed on the dead bodies of animals or men.

43 *As we were sickly prey* – "as if we were ready to die (*sickly*) and become their food (*prey*)".

44 *lies, ready to give up the ghost* – "lies (as if ill in bed, under the canopy or bed-hanging), at the point of death".

Roman standards

BRUTUS

Ho, Lucilius, hark, a word with you!   70

LUCILIUS

My lord?

> [*Standing forth. He and* BRUTUS *converse apart*

CASSIUS

Messala!

MESSALA

[*Standing forth*] What says my general?

CASSIUS

Messala, this is my birth-day, as this very day
Was Cassius born. Give me thy hand, Messala:
Be thou my witness,³⁴ that against my will   75
As Pompey was,³⁵ am I compelled to set
Upon one battle all our liberties.³⁶
You know that I held Epicurus strong,
And his opinion.³⁷ Now I change my mind,
And partly credit things that do presage.³⁸   80
Coming from Sardis, on our former ensign
Two mighty eagles fell,³⁹ and there they perched,
Gorging and feeding from our soldiers' hands,
Who to Philippi here consorted us.⁴⁰
This morning are they fled away, and gone,   85
And in their steads⁴¹ do ravens, crows and kites⁴²
Fly o'er our heads, and downward look on us
As we were sickly prey;⁴³ their shadows seem
A canopy most fatal, under which
Our army lies, ready to give up the ghost.⁴⁴   90

MESSALA

Believe not so.

45 *I but believe it partly* – "I only
believe it in part".
46 *fresh of spirit* – "cheerful in mind".
47 *very constantly* – "without fear or
hesitation".
48 *The gods today stand friendly . . .
befall* – "May the gods today be
firm in their favour (*stand friendly*)
to us, so that we may as friends
when the war is over (*Lovers in
peace*) live on to old age. But, since
the things that can happen to men
(*the affairs of men*) remain always
(*rest still*) uncertain, let us take into
account (*reason with*) the worst that
can happen (*befall*)".

49 *by the rule of that philosophy* – "I
shall act according to (*by*) the teach-
ing of that philosophy . . ." Brutus
is probably speaking of the Stoic
philosophy that a man should
endure all suffering calmly. Cato
killed himself after Pompey's
defeat, so as not to fall into the
hands of Caesar.
50 *For fear . . . time of life* – "out of fear
of what might happen, to stop the
course of one's life by suicide".
51 *arming myself with patience . . . below*
– "making myself strong and
patient to live through (*stay*) what
is decided for me (*the providence*) by
the gods who govern men of this
earth below".
52 *You are contented . . . Thorough the
streets* – "you agree to be led in the
procession of triumph (of Antony
and Octavius) through the streets",
i.e. led as a captive.
53 *bound* – "in chains".

CASSIUS

I but believe it partly,[45]
For I am fresh of spirit,[46] and resolved
To meet all perils, very constantly.[47]

BRUTUS

Even so, Lucilius.

CASSIUS

Now, most noble Brutus,
The gods today stand friendly, that we may,   95
Lovers in peace, lead on our days to age!
But since the affairs of men rest still incertain,
Let 's reason with the worst that may befall.[48]
If we do lose this battle, then is this
The very last time we shall speak together: 100
What are you then determinéd to do?

BRUTUS

Even by the rule of that philosophy,[49]
By which I did blame Cato for the death
Which he did give himself, – I know not how,
But I do find it cowardly and vile,   105
For fear of what might fall, so to prevent
The time of life,[50] – arming myself with patience,
To stay the providence of some high Powers,
That govern us below.[51]

CASSIUS

Then, if we lose this battle,   110
You are contented to be led in triumph[52]
Thorough the streets of Rome.

BRUTUS

No, Cassius, no. Think not, thou noble Roman,
That ever Brutus will go bound[53] to Rome,

SUMMARY OF ACT V SCENE 2

1 The forces of Brutus attack those of Octavius and are victorious.

2 *Alarum.* The signal to start the battle.

3 *bills* – "written papers".

4 *set on* – "attack".

5 *But cold demeanour . . . the overthrow* – "only faint courage in the men led by Octavius, and a sudden sharp attack will defeat them".

He bears too great a mind. But this same day   115
Must end that work the Ides of March began.
And whether we shall meet again I know not:
Therefore our everlasting farewell take:
For ever, and for ever, farewell Cassius!
If we do meet again, why, we shall smile;   120
If not, why then, this parting was well made.

CASSIUS

For ever, and for ever, farewell, Brutus:
If we do meet again, we 'll smile indeed;
If not, 't is true, this parting was well made.

BRUTUS

Why then lead on. O that a man might know   125
The end of this day's business, ere it come:
But it sufficeth that the day will end,
And then the end is known. Come ho, away!

                               [Exeunt

Scene II. The field of battle.[1]
Alarum.[2] *Enter* BRUTUS *and* MESSALA.

BRUTUS

Ride, ride, Messala, ride and give these bills[3]
Unto the legions on the other side.

                            [Loud alarum

Let them set on[4] at once; for I perceive
But cold demeanour in Octavius' wing,
And sudden push gives them the overthrow.[5]   5
Ride, ride, Messala, let them all come down.

                               [Exeunt

SUMMARY OF ACT V SCENE 3

1 The forces of Cassius are surrounded by those of Antony. Brutus has advanced too hastily. Titinius is sent to find out what is going on in another part of the battlefield. Pindarus thinks he sees him captured: he kills Cassius, as Cassius asks. Titinius returns to find Cassius dead. Brutus is given the news. Another attack is yet to be made by Brutus' army.

2 *the villains fly . . . enemy* – "the wicked men (of our own side) are running away! I have turned and fought against soldiers of my own side".

3 *ensign* – "standard-bearer".

4 *it* – "the flag".

5 *the word* – "the order to attack".

6 *Who having some advantage . . . enclosed* – "and when he found himself rather stronger than Octavius he took the opportunity (*advantage*) too readily; his soldiers began to (*fell to*) take plunder while we are quite surrounded (*all enclosed*) by Antony's soldiers".

7 *and hide thy spurs in him* – "and ride fast (spurring on the horse until the spurs are hidden in his flesh)".

Scene III. Another part of the field.[1]
Alarums. Enter CASSIUS *and* TITINIUS.

CASSIUS

O, look, Titinius, look, the villains fly!
Myself have to mine own turned enemy;[2]
This ensign[3] here of mine was turning back,
I slew the coward, and did take it[4] from him.

TITINIUS

O Cassius, Brutus gave the word[5] too early,   5
Who having some advantage on Octavius,
Took it too eagerly; his soldiers fell to spoil,
Whilst we by Antony are all enclosed.[6]

Enter PINDARUS

PINDARUS

Fly further off, my lord; fly further off!
Mark Antony is in your tents, my lord.   10
Fly therefore, noble Cassius, fly far off!

CASSIUS

This hill is far enough. Look, look, Titinius!
Are those my tents where I perceive the fire?

TITINIUS

They are, my lord.

CASSIUS

        Titinius, if thou lovest me,
Mount thou my horse, and hide thy spurs in him,[7]   15
Till he have brought thee up to yonder troops
And here again, that I may rest assured
Whether yond troops are friend or enemy.

8 *with a thought* – "with the speed of thought".

9 *My sight . . . Titinius* – "my sight was never clear. Keep your eyes on Titinius".

10 *I breathéd first* – "I was born".

11 *My life is run his compass* – "My life has made its circle, from beginning to end".

12 *that make . . . spur* – "who are galloping towards him" (*on the spur*, 'quickly').

13 *light* – "get down from their horses".

14 *I swore thee, saving of thy life* – "I made you promise on oath when I spared your life . . ."

TITINIUS

I will be here again, even with a thought. [8]

[*Exit*

CASSIUS

Go, Pindarus, get higher on that hill·   20
My sight was ever thick. Regard Titinius, [9]
And tell me what thou not'st about the field.

[*Exit* PINDARUS

This day I breathéd first. [10] Time is come round,
And where I did begin, there shall I end;
My life is run his compass. [11] Sirrah, what news?   25

PINDARUS

[*Above*] O, my lord!

CASSIUS

What news?

PINDARUS

Titinius is encloséd round about
With horsemen, that make to him on the spur; [12]
Yet he spurs on. Now they are almost on him!   30
Now, Titinius. Now, some light. [13] O, he lights too.
He 's ta'en. [*Shout*] And hark, they shout for joy.

CASSIUS

Come down; behold no more!
O coward that I am, to live so long,
To see my best friend ta'en before my face.   35

[PINDARUS *comes down*

Come hither, sirrah.
In Parthia did I take thee prisoner,
And then I swore thee, saving of thy life, [14]
That whatsoever I did bid thee do,

233

15 *be a free-man* – "in return you shall be no longer a slave".
16 *bowels* – "entrails".
17 *search this bosom* – "stab my chest".
18 *Stand not to answer* – "Do not stop to reply".
19 *Durst I have done my will* – "if I had dared to do as I wished".
20 *take note of him* – "see him".
21 *but change* – "only an interchange of victory and defeat".
22 *These tidings . . . Cassius* – "This news will give fresh strength to Cassius" (*comfort*, 'to strengthen').
23 *All disconsolate* – "Quite without hope".

Thou shouldst attempt it. Come now, keep thine oath, 40
Now be a free-man;[15] and with this good sword
That ran through Caesar's bowels,[16] search this bosom.[17]
Stand not to answer.[18] Here, take thou the hilts,
And when my face is covered, as 't is now,
Guide thou the sword. [PINDARUS *stabs him*] Caesar, thou art
 revenged, 45
Even with the sword that killéd thee!   *[Dies*

PINDARUS

So, I am free; yet would not so have been,
Durst I have done my will.[19] O Cassius,
Far from this country Pindarus shall run,
Where never Roman shall take note of him![20] 50

          [Exit

Re-enter TITINIUS *with* MESSALA

MESSALA

It is but change,[21] Titinius: for Octavius
Is overthrown by noble Brutus' power,
As Cassius' legions are by Antony.

TITINIUS

These tidings will well comfort Cassius.[22]

MESSALA

Where did you leave him?

TITINIUS

    All disconsolate,[23] 55
With Pindarus, his bondman, on this hill.

MESSALA

Is not that he that lies upon the ground?

24 *He lies . . . living* – "He is not lying as a living man would lie".

25 *our deeds are done* – "our great deeds are finished".

26 *Mistrust of my success . . . deed* – "His lack of confidence (*Mistrust*) in what I was doing (*of my success*) caused this suicide".

27 *of good success* – "in victory".

28 *O hateful Error . . . that art not* – "What a hideous mistake (*hateful Error*) born of, or caused by, sorrow (*Melancholy*) that makes men who are ready (*apt*) to do so, believe what is not true!"

29 *O Error, soon conceived . . . engendered thee* – "Such a mistake, received too quickly (*soon*) into the mind, can never have a good result, but brings about death (just as a baby may kill its mother as it is born)!" (*Conceive*, 'to think', also 'to conceive a child'; *engender*, 'to bear'.)

30 *darts envenoméd* – "poisoned sharp points".

31 *As tidings of this sight* – "as news of what we have seen".

TITINIUS

He lies not like the living.[24] O my heart!

MESSALA

Is not that he?

TITINIUS

      No, this was he, Messala,
But Cassius is no more. O setting sun: 60
As in thy red rays thou dost sink tonight,
So in his red blood Cassius' day is set.
The sun of Rome is set. Our day is gone;
Clouds, dews, and dangers come; our deeds are done.[25]
Mistrust of my success hath done this deed.[26]   65

MESSALA

Mistrust of good success[27] hath done this deed.
O hateful Error, Melancholy's child:
Why dost thou show to the apt thoughts of men
The things that are not?[28] O Error, soon conceived,
Thou never comest unto a happy birth,   70
But killst the mother that engendered thee.[29]

TITINIUS

What, Pindarus? Where art thou, Pindarus?

MESSALA

Seek him, Titinius, whilst I go to meet
The noble Brutus, thrusting this report
Into his ears; I may say, thrusting it;   75
For piercing steel, and darts envenoméd,[30]
Shall be as welcome to the ears of Brutus
As tidings of this sight.[31]

32 *apace* – "quickly".
33 *how I regarded* – "how I found and how I showed respect to . . ." (*regard*, 'to see' and 'to show regard for').

34 *a Roman's part* – "a true Roman's duty".
35 *upward* – "upturned".

Put on my brows this wreath of victory

TITINIUS

Hie you, Messala,
And I will seek for Pindarus the while.

[Exit MESSALA

Why didst thou send me forth, brave Cassius?   80
Did I not meet thy friends, and did not they
Put on my brows this wreath of victory,
And bid me give it thee? Didst thou not hear their shouts?
Alas, thou hast misconstrued every thing.
But hold thee, take this garland on thy brow;   85
Thy Brutus bid me give it thee, and I
Will do his bidding. Brutus, come apace,[32]
And see how I regarded[33] Caius Cassius:
By your leave, gods. This is a Roman's part![34]
Come Cassius' sword, and find Titinius' heart!   90

[Kills himself

Alarum. Re-enter MESSALA *with* BRUTUS, *young* CATO,
STRATO, VOLUMNIUS, LUCILIUS, *and* others.

BRUTUS

Where, where, Messala, doth his body lie?

MESSALA

Lo, yonder, and Titinius mourning it.

BRUTUS

Titinius' face is upward.[35]

CATO

He is slain!

239

36 *proper* – "own, individual".
37 *breed thy fellow* – "bring forth any
to equal you".
38 *moe* – "more".
39 *discomfort* – "weaken and sadden".
40 *field* – "field of battle".
41 *set our battles on* – "order our men
to begin the fight".

1 Brutus and his men are hard-pressed in battle. Lucilius pretends to be
Brutus and is captured. Antony spares his life.

2 *yet hold up your heads !* – "still fight
bravely!"

BRUTUS

O Julius Caesar, thou art mighty, yet,
Thy spirit walks abroad, and turns our **swords** 95
In our own proper[36] entrails!

[Low alarums

CATO

Brave Titinius,
Look whe'er he have not crowned dead Cassius.

BRUTUS

Are yet two Romans living such as these?
The last of all the Romans, fare thee well!
It is impossible that ever Rome 100
Should breed thy fellow.[37] Friends, I owe moe[38] **tears**
To this dead man than you shall see me pay.
I shall find time, Cassius; I shall find time.
Come therefore, and to Thasos send his body;
His funerals shall not be in our camp, 105
Lest it discomfort[39] us. Lucilius, come,
And come, young Cato, let us to the field![40]
Labeo and Flavius set our battles on![41]
'T is three o'clock, and, Romans, yet ere night,
We shall try fortune in a second fight. 110

[Exeunt

Scene IV. Another part of the field.[1]
Alarum. Enter, fighting, Soldiers *of both armies; then* BRUTUS,
young CATO, LUCILIUS *and others.*

BRUTUS

Yet, countrymen, O yet, hold up your heads![2]

241

3 *What bastard doth not?* – "Only a man who is not truly Roman will fail to fight" (*bastard*, one of dishonourable birth).

4 *Only I yield to die* – "I give in only on condition that you kill me".

CATO

What bastard doth not?³ Who will go with me?
I will proclaim my name about the field.
I am the son of Marcus Cato, ho,
A foe to tyrants, and my country's friend!   5
I am the son of Marcus Cato, ho!

Enter soldiers, *and fight*

BRUTUS

And I am Brutus, Marcus Brutus, I,
Brutus, my country's friend. Know me for Brutus!

[*Exit*

LUCILIUS

O young and noble Cato, art thou down?
Why, now thou diest, as bravely as Titinius,   10
And mayst be honoured, being Cato's son.

I SOLDIER

Yield, or thou diest.

LUCILIUS

Only I yield to die.⁴
[*Offering money*] There is so much that thou wilt kill me
    straight:
Kill Brutus, and be honoured in his death.

I SOLDIER

We must not: a noble prisoner!   15

2 SOLDIER

Room, ho! Tell Antony, Brutus is ta'en.

5 *is chanced* -"has turned out".

1 Brutus dies on his own sword to escape capture. Antony and Octavius speak of his great nobility.

I SOLDIER

I 'll tell the news. Here comes the General!

Enter ANTONY

Brutus is ta'en, Brutus is ta'en, my lord!

ANTONY

Where is he?

LUCILIUS

Safe, Antony. Brutus is safe enough.   20
I dare assure thee that no enemy
Shall ever take alive the noble Brutus.
The gods defend him from so great a shame!
When you do find him, or alive, or dead,
He will be found like Brutus, like himself.   25

ANTONY

This is not Brutus, friend, but, I assure you,
A prize no less in worth. Keep this man safe,
Give him all kindness. I had rather have
Such men my friends than enemies. Go on,
And see whe'er Brutus be alive or dead,   30
And bring us word, unto Octavius' tent
How every thing is chanced.[5]

[*Exeunt*

Scene V. Another part of the field.[1]
Enter BRUTUS, DARDANIUS, CLITUS, STRATO, *and*
VOLUMNIUS.

BRUTUS

Come, poor remains of friends, rest on this rock.

245

2 *showed the torch-light*. Statilius, a
soldier of Brutus, who had gone to
find out what was happening in
another part of the battlefield, had
given the agreed signal of their
success by lifting up a lighted
torch.

246

CLITUS

Statilius showed the torch-light,[2] but, my lord,
He came not back: he is or ta'en or slain.

BRUTUS

Sit thee down, Clitus; slaying is the word;
It is a deed in fashion. Hark thee, Clitus.   5

CLITUS

What, I, my lord? No, not for all the world.

BRUTUS

Peace then, no words.

CLITUS

I 'll rather kill myself.

BRUTUS

Hark thee, Dardanius.

DARDANIUS

Shall I do such a deed?

CLITUS

O, Dardanius!

DARDANIUS

O, Clitus!   10

CLITUS

What ill request did Brutus make to thee?

DARDANIUS

To kill him, Clitus; look, he meditates.

3 *noble vessel*. Brutus is compared to a splendid drinking-vessel overflowing with grief.
4 *list* – "listen . . ."
5 *several* – "separate".
6 *hour* – "hour of death".

7 *Thou seest the world . . . to the pit* – "You see how the world is moving. Our foes have beaten us back to the edge of the deep pit of death".
8 *tarry* – "wait, stay".

CLITUS

Now is that noble vessel full of grief[3]
That it runs over even at his eyes.

BRUTUS

Come hither, good Volumnius, list[4] a word.   15

VOLUMNIUS

What says my lord?

BRUTUS

          Why, this, Volumnius:
The ghost of Caesar hath appeared to me
Two several[5] times by night: at Sardis, once;
And this last night, here in Philippi fields:
I know my hour[6] is come.

VOLUMNIUS

          Not so, my lord.   20

BRUTUS

Nay, I am sure it is, Volumnius.
Thou seest the world, Volumnius, how it goes,
Our enemies have beat us to the pit:[7]   [Low alarums
It is more worthy to leap in ourselves
Than tarry[8] till they push us. Good Volumnius,   25
Thou knowst that we two went to school together:
Even for that our love of old, I prithee
Hold thou my sword hilts whilst I run on it.

VOLUMNIUS

That 's not an office for a friend, my lord.

          [Alarum still

249

9 *My heart doth joy . . . shall attain unto* – "my heart feels glad that up to now (*yet*), in all my life, I have never met (*found*) a man who was nòt loyal to me. I shall win fame from this lost battle (*this losing day*) greater than Octavius and Mark Antony shall gain (*attain unto*) by shameful victory (*vile conquest*) over me".

10 *Night hangs . . . this hour* – "My eyes are heavy with sleep; my body, which has struggled for nothing else than to reach this hour of death, wishes for rest".

11 *respect* – "reputation".

12 *smatch* – "taste, amount".

250

CLITUS

Fly, fly, my lord, there is no tarrying here.   30

BRUTUS

Farewell to you, and you, and you, Volumnius.
Strato, thou hast been all this while asleep:
Farewell to thee too, Strato. Countrymen,
My heart doth joy, that yet in all my life,
I found no man but he was true to me.   35
I shall have glory by this losing day
More than Octavius and Mark Antony,
By this vile conquest, shall attain unto.⁹
So fare you well at once, for Brutus' tongue
Hath almost ended his life's history.   40
Night hangs upon mine eyes; my bones would rest,
That have but laboured to attain this hour.¹⁰

[*Alarum. Cry within "Fly, fly, fly!"*

CLITUS

Fly, my lord, fly!

BRUTUS

Hence! I will follow.

[*Exeunt* CLITUS, DARDANIUS, *and* VOLUMNIUS

I prithee, Strato, stay thou by thy lord;
Thou art a fellow of a good respect.¹¹   45
Thy life hath had some smatch¹² of honour in it.
Hold then my sword, and turn away thy face,
While I do run upon it. Wilt thou, Strato?

STRATO

Give me your hand first. Fare you well, my lord.

13 *Caesar, now be still . . . will* – "Now Caesar, you may be content. I did not kill you half so willingly as I kill myself".

14 *man* – "servant".

15 *Free from the bondage . . . overcame himself* – "Not a prisoner as you are, Messala. Those who have won the battle can do no more than light a funeral fire with his body, for no one but Brutus conquered Brutus".

16 *So Brutus should be found* – "It is right that we should find Brutus dead in this way".

17 *Lucilius' saying.* See v.iv.21.

18 *All that served . . . with me?* – "All the servants of Brutus I will take into my service and treat them well. Young man, will you spend your days in my service?"

19 *prefer* – "recommend".

BRUTUS

Farewell, good Strato. [*Runs on his sword*] Caesar, now be still! 50
I killed not thee with half so good a will.[13]   [*Dies*

[*Alarum. Retreat. Enter* OCTAVIUS, ANTONY,
MESSALA, LUCILIUS *and the* Army

OCTAVIUS

What man is that?

MESSALA

My master's man.[14] Strato, where is thy master?

STRATO

Free from the bondage you are in, Messala.
The conquerors can but make a fire of him,   55
For Brutus only overcame himself,[15]
And no man else hath honour by his death.

LUCILIUS

So Brutus should be found![16] I thank thee, Brutus,
That thou hast proved Lucilius' saying[17] true.

OCTAVIUS

All that served Brutus, I will entertain them.   60
Fellow, wilt thou bestow thy time with me?[18]

STRATO

Ay, if Messala will prefer[19] me to you.

OCTAVIUS

Do so, good Messala.

MESSALA

How died my master, Strato?

253

20 *save only he* – "except himself only".
21 *that they did* – "what they did".
22 *He only . . . one of them* – "Brutus alone joined the conspirators out of a sincere wish (*honest thought*) for the good of Rome (*general*) and her people".
23 *gentle* – "noble".
24 *elements.* It was believed that all things were made out of the four 'elements' or earliest forms of matter – earth, air, fire and water. Nature had so made Brutus that she could truly claim to have made a noble man.

25 *virtue* – "nobility".
26 *let us use . . . rites of burial* – "let us treat him with all honour and give him the proper funeral service".
27 *Most like . . . honourably* – "as is most fitting for a soldier, with everything nobly arranged".
28 *So call the field . . . happy day* – "So sound the end of the battle and let us go to decide what fame and honour every man has won in this victory" (*part*, 'to share').

STRATO

I held the sword, and he did run on it.   65

MESSALA

Octavius then, take him to follow thee,
That did the latest service to my master.

ANTONY

This was the noblest Roman of them all.
All the conspirators save only he,[20]
Did that they did[21] in envy of great Caesar.   70
He only, in a general honest thought,
And common good to all, made one of them.[22]
His life was gentle,[23] and the elements[24]
So mixed in him that nature might stand up,
And say to all the world "This was a man!"   75

OCTAVIUS

According to his virtue,[25] let us use him
With all respect and rites of burial.[26]
Within my tent his bones tonight shall lie,
Most like a soldier, ordered honourably.[27]
So call the field to rest, and let 's away,   80
To part the glories of this happy day.[28]

[*Exeunt*

SOME ADVICE FOR EXAMINATION CANDIDATES

Begin your examination by reading through the question paper slowly and thoughtfully. Then decide on which of the questions you are going to answer, making quite sure you have chosen the right number, and that they come from the right sections of the paper.

As you begin to plan your answers, make absolutely certain you are answering the question on the paper; do not write something else; *do exactly what the question asks you to do.*

Examiners use a number of *types* of question on Shakespeare's plays. Here are examples of five different types, with some suggestions as to how each of them should be answered. Your teacher will tell you which types of question are likely to come up in the examination you are taking.

1 You are given a number of *short passages* taken from the play and are asked to write answers to questions on one or more of them. The questions generally refer only to the given passage itself and its immediate surroundings, its 'context', in the play. Choose the passage(s) you know best and make certain you answer every question you are asked about it/them.

For example:

> Yet Brutus says he was ambitious,
> And Brutus is an honourable man.
> You all did see that, on the Lupercal,
> I thrice presented him a kingly crown,
> Which he did thrice refuse. Was this ambition?
> Yet Brutus says he was ambitious,
> And, sure, he is an honourable man.
> I speak not to disprove what Brutus spoke,
> But here I am, to speak what I do know.
> You all did love him once, not without cause;
> What cause withholds you then to mourn for him?
> *O judgement! Thou art fled to brutish beasts,*
> *And men have lost their reason!*

257

(i)   State *two* examples of Caesar's lack of ambition mentioned before this speech.
(ii) Does Antony really believe at this point that Brutus is 'honourable'? Why does he keep using this word to describe him?
(iii) What does Antony intend to achieve through this speech?
(iv) What is the significance of the words in italics?

(from West African Examinations Council, School Certificate and G.C.E., November, 1981.)

SUGGESTED ANSWERS

(The passage quoted is at III.ii 90–102.)

(i)   Before his attack of the 'falling sickness', Caesar bared his throat and offered it to the crowd to cut. After his attack, he asked the crowd to put down to his sickness anything he had done or said amiss. (Cassius says Caesar would not be a lion if the Romans had more spirit, if they were not as frightened as deer – I.iii.107.)

(ii) No, he uses the word 'honourable' ironically, suggesting that his opinion of Caesar is the same as the crowd's, but implying just the opposite, that he considers Brutus totally *dis*honourable, wicked. He keeps on using the word 'honourable' so as to make the crowd think about it and realise it is not to be taken at face value.

(iii) He wants to win the crowd's sympathy for the dead Caesar, and so make them turn against the murderers.

(iv) 'Good sense! You have deserted men and have gone to senseless, savage animals instead.' (He implies that the crowd would not praise Brutus and the other conspirators if they used their sense.)

2 You are given *a longer passage* from the play and have to answer questions on it. The passage may be printed in full on the examination paper, or you may be given a copy of the play for use at the examination. If you are given a plain text of the play, you will be asked to find the required passage in it; in this case, make absolutely sure you find the right passage, where it begins and where it ends. Some of the questions which follow the passage are likely to refer to its setting in the play as a whole, not just to details of the passage itself and its immediate surroundings.

For example, the passage set is II.ii. lines 26–49 (p. 87 in *New Swan*), from
CAESAR   What can be avoided ...
to:

                  ... And Caesar shall go forth.

258

(i)   Give details of 'the predictions' to which Caesar refers.

(ii) Identify two aspects of Caesar's character as revealed in this passage. State your evidence.

(iii) Explain:

> Cowards die many times before their deaths;
> The valiant never taste of death but once.

(iv) Summarise Calpurnia's dream and Decius's explanation of it, and show how he persuades Caesar to go to the Senate.

(from London University G.C.E., O-level, Eng. Lit. Syllabus A, June 1980)

SUGGESTED ANSWERS

(i)   There has been a storm of thunder and lightning during the previous night which is not yet over.

During the night, Calpurnia, Caesar's wife, cried out 'Help, ho! They murder Caesar'. She dreamt that his statue ran blood like a fountain, and the Romans bathed their hands in it.

Someone has reported extraordinary events: a lioness has whelped in the streets of the city; graves have opened and let out their dead; apparitions of fighting men shone out from the clouds as if they were lined up for war, so that blood fell like soft rain down on the Capitol; the air was filled with the noise of battle, horses neighing, dying men groaning; ghosts shrieked and squealed in the streets.

(ii) Caesar is genuinely brave despite his physical weaknesses. In a society and an age which believed unquestioningly in a supernatural power which influenced men's lives, he puts his personal bravery above the danger threatening him; he says about himself:

'Danger knows full well/That Caesar is more dangerous than he'.

He is a thinker as well as a doer. He sees his own courage as preferable to the coward's belief in fate: the coward is always dogged by fears of death, whereas he, Caesar, takes pride in his bravery, and is not frightened by the knowledge that eventually he will die. 'It seems to me most strange that men should fear,/Seeing that death ... /Will come when it will come'.

(iii) In their own imagination, cowards 'die' many times over before their real death occurs; the brave man experiences death only once.

(iv) Calpurnia dreamt she saw Caesar's statue running with pure blood, like a fountain with a hundred spouts; many lusty Romans came up to it smiling, and bathed their hands in it.

Decius denies her interpretation of it (doubtless as a symbol of Caesar's body gushing blood from many wounds), and asserts it was

259

a favourable omen. It signified that Rome would go on to suck reviving blood from Caesar; great men would gather around him to get a piece of his clothing stained with his blood, and keep it as a holy relic, and as a mark of honour for display.

Decius says that Caesar will be crowned king if he goes to the Senate that day. If Caesar now sends a message to say he has decided not to come, the Senators may change their minds and not make him king after all. Besides, they would mock him if the truth got out and someone could say he would not be at the Senate until his wife had better dreams. And if he then hid, they would say Caesar was afraid. To avoid these slights, Caesar must go.

3 You are asked to write an essay on certain *aspects of a character* in the play. You are *not* required to tell this character's story; you are to write about the character from a particular point of view.

For example: 'A shrewd observer of the political scene, not a mere embittered plotter.' Do you agree with this description of Cassius? Illustrate your answer with close reference to the text.

(from West African Examinations Council, School Certificate/G.C.E., November, 1982)

In planning your answer to this question, you should first think quickly through the play, and note down in rough some key words which describe Cassius at various stages in the development of the plot. You should not expect him to appear as constant in his behaviour and attitudes throughout the play: he is consistently jealous of Caesar's power and achievement; but he is sometimes firmer in purpose than Brutus is, and only later gives into him in important matters. The evidence you need in order to support the impression of Cassius, as you note it in the key words, will be taken from what Cassius says about himself, what others say about him, and what can be reasonably inferred from the situations and events in the play as a whole.

Here are a few descriptive terms about him which might form the basis of a full answer; each term is followed by a few notes referring to supporting evidence in the play. Your answer will of course need to be written out in full, as an extended essay with each of your points fully explained, and supported by detailed reference to places in the text. (You will not be expected to indicate in your essay the number of the act or scene you take your evidence from; a reference to its place in the plot is quite sufficient.) On the basis of the description you have worked out, you must give your opinion on the quotation: you are not compelled to agree with it – indeed you may totally *disagree* – but once having made up your mind about it, make sure you state your view plainly, and keep to this view once you have decided on it.

He thinks too much – Caesar's famous words about him suggest he is a shrewd observer, but how far are his thoughts political, i.e. connected with the state?

a plotter – he wants to do something about the ambitious Caesar, yet he declares that if Caesar is offered the crown, he (Cassius) will liberate himself from this bondage by taking his own life – hardly a *political* gesture (I.iii.89ff); but does he do this so as to have his views reported to Caesar, or is he sincere in saying his concern is with that part of the tyranny which he is to bear? When he begins to move the conspiracy against Caesar, he seems to be motivated by personal *jealousy*, a *totally embittered view* of all that Caesar stands for (I.iii.104ff.)

From this point onwards he assembles fellow-conspirators around him, most notably Brutus, yet does not appeal to them on grounds of advantage to the state and the freedom and welfare of its citizens.

Perhaps only in III.i. does he come near to political shrewdness. In two places here (148–150, 247) he questions Brutus's keenness to get Antony back, and his wisdom in allowing Antony to speak at Caesar's funeral. But even here Cassius may have uppermost in his mind his own personal safety as a conspirator, and only below this Antony's rise to power and influence.

His other qualities are evidently directed inwards: he is *greedy* – he has an 'itching palm' (IV.iii.10), and is able to use money to serve his own ends, e.g. in levying powers;

impetuous – Brutus warns him against being uncertain when the time comes to assassinate Caesar (III.i.22); he even forfeits his own life (something he has talked about before – I.iii.89–90, III.i.22) before his defeat is certain, on the grounds that his friend Titinius, sent to another part of the field to find out what is going on, seemed to have been taken by the enemy. When Titinius returns safely, with news of a victory won by Brutus and his forces, he says to Cassius, lying dead, 'Alas, thou hast misconstrued every thing' (V.iii.84).

superstitious – he is dogged by the thought that the battle of Philippi is to be fought on his birth-day (V.i.73, V.iii.23)

It therefore seems, in our view at least, that Cassius is well described as

261

an 'embittered plotter', but, contrary to the view of the given quotation, is not shown in the play as 'a shrewd observer of the political scene'. It looks as if Brutus is quite right when he says (II.i.61), 'Since Cassius first did whet me against Caesar', not '. . . whet me against tyranny, dictatorship', since Cassius hated the man, not the political system he was set to introduce.

4 Questions are sometimes based on a *major aspect, feature or theme* of the play, often by quoting something a critic has written about it, and then asking you to comment on this quotation.

For example: The play has been called a 'political thriller'. With close attention to the text, say how far you consider this an apt description.
(from London University, G.C.E., O-level, January 1981)

As with the previous question (No. 3 above), the starting-point in planning an answer must be to think carefully through the play with a particular aspect of it in mind, in this case its alleged similarity to a political thriller. Again we must emphasise that you are in no way required to agree with the suggestion that this is an apt description of *Julius Caesar*. Indeed we shall try to show in the following notes that we do *not* consider it a very apt description, though to consider the play in this light helps us to get to know and appreciate it more profoundly.

What are the essentials of a political thriller? We think it must be a story which involves our emotions, especially the emotion of intense curiosity as to how the story will work out in the end. It gives the evidence of situations and events which usually lead up to someone committing a crime, and the reader is led through a series of enquiries so as to find out who committed it. The whole story is expected to be exciting and sensational. As for 'political', such a story would merit this description if it dealt with people in government and in high places in society, unlike, say, the thrillers about Sherlock Holmes or Perry Mason or Inspector Poirot.

Assuming that you can agree with the way we have identified a political thriller, your task is now to see how far *Julius Caesar* can be said to fit into this category of fiction.

Is it political? Well, certainly. Caesar himself is the greatest man of his time, poised to set up an empire which will be the most powerful and extensive of the ancient world, and a dynasty through his nephew

Octavius. Around him, when he is back in Rome from triumphs elsewhere, he gathers large numbers of political associates, enemies as well as friends, all of them, even Calpurnia and Portia and the poets, involved in some way or other in the political life of the state.

Is it a thriller? Well, perhaps less so. No one would deny that it stirs our emotions with excitement and a sensation of pending disaster. The cobbler's jokes at the beginning might suggest otherwise – the wordplay sounds like the start of a comedy, but it is all there for a serious purpose: this is how the crowd is likely to behave and in this way affect the train of events started by Caesar's return in triumph. Up to the middle of the play, things happen in quick, exciting succession, until Caesar lies dead, assassinated because many men with power and influence have realised he would aim at overthrowing the republic and establishing a dictatorship. Cassius at least was motivated to start the conspiracy out of personal jealousy and resentment.

There is some uncertainty as to what will happen: will Caesar go to the Senate House despite the warnings and portents (II.ii–iv)? What are Antony's true motives for addressing the crowd? Is he totally sincere, or has he other, hidden ends (see especially III.ii.254f)? – and so on. But unlike the general run of thrillers, we all know who the murderers are; in the rest of the play, no process of discovery is involved.

What is there instead? Essentially, the flight of the two chief conspirators, Brutus and Cassius, and what happens to their alliance; and the rise of Antony, who, with Octavius (Caesar's nephew and adoptive son, and the future Emperor Augustus) and the light-weight Lepidus, plans the division of the Roman world between the three of them. The battle between these leaders at Philippi and its results, in the death of Brutus and the strengthening of Antony's faction, are where the play ends. All this is hardly like the resolution of the thriller, but rather the dramatisation of the consequences of Caesar's assassination.

You will of course be expected to write a connected essay in answer to this question. The notes here are an indication of how you should think through all the key aspects of the question, and do not attempt to give the sort of connected piece about the matter which your examiners will be looking for. It is very important also to remember, all through, that they want to know your opinion of the given idea; make sure you *have* an opinion (not necessarily the one expressed above), and that you keep to it throughout your answer, and give evidence which supports it consistently.

5 Your teacher may have been working with you mainly on *producing* the play for the stage. If so, he or she will be giving you a good idea of what you are likely to be asked in your examination. However, you may find the following hints useful.

Questions will probably be on the same lines as this one:
'Imagine you are working on a production of *Julius Caesar*.
How would you direct . . . ? What especially would you want to convey to your audience in this part of the play?'

In planning your answer, your first job is to try to visualise what has to happen on the stage, i.e. what are the essentials laid down in the text of the play. Write some rough notes about these essentials so that you keep them in your mind while you are setting down the details of what you would do as a director. Do *not* write out the story of the play, or the part of it referred to in the question: your examiners will know the plot already, and if you just retell it you will not be answering their question.

We have chosen III.i, the assassination scene, to illustrate the sort of approach we recommend, and we note below a number of notions about the production of this scene which you will need to consider. Under each heading you will find some questions to think about; your decisions on such questions will make up the body of your answer.

This long scene contains the climax of the play; in it, the god-like rise of Caesar is brought to a sudden halt, and the rise of Antony begins. But although its place in the structure of the play is easily stated, it is by no means easy to direct, largely because of two basic problems it raises for the producer. First is the handling of the crowd. At the beginning of the scene a crowd has assembled, including some minor characters named in the play as well as others. How are the key characters to be brought out so that your audience has a clear notion of who is important and where the action is going to lie? You cannot expect your audience to remember the names of all the minor characters or to distinguish them from the major ones without help, especially when the major ones do not use names in addressing one another. Second, and arising from the first, to what extent is the actual death of Caesar to be highlighted? It is after all the focal point of the scene, yet we must not lose sight of the fact that by choice he has boldly mixed with the people; to further his ambitions, so much depends on carrying them with him. Even when, on-stage, he moves up into the Senate-house (line 12), he is not to become an isolated figure, remote from the rest, but is still with the crowd who move with him. Near the end of the scene, when Antony is left alone with Caesar's body, the servant who arrives from Octavius does not immediately notice it and delivers some of his message first (283ff). The quiet ending is to be made at once a culmination (Brutus tells Antony to take the body – 248) and also a working-out of what was foreseen and becomes an immense tragedy: civil war and the great shift of power away from the republicans (Antony and the servant together carry Caesar's body away).

Costumes and make-up
One way, perhaps the most straightforward and therefore the best, of solving the problem of identification is to dress the key conspirators with some modest distinguishing mark, say a coloured fringe to their togas. This proposal assumes, of course, that you are dressing the characters in a form of ancient Roman costume, a mode not always implied in the play – witness the illustrations on pp. 28, 30 and 222. At any rate, some device or other in their dress could be used to direct attention towards seven of the characters (Brutus, Cassius, Casca, Decius, Metellus, Trebonius, Cinna), forming a group counterbalanced by Caesar, who will be distinguished anyway by what happens to him, and by Antony, whose allegiances at this point are uncertain. But of course such marking needs to be discreet since the last thing the conspirators will want to do is to identify themselves in the eyes of Caesar as an alliance or power group. Or do you consider that Antony (alone?) should have some contrasting mark?

As regards make-up, there are plenty of indications throughout the play as to the relative ages of the major characters, e.g. of Cassius and Brutus at iv.iii.30f.

The stage set
The scene directions are precise: something integral to the set must represent the outside of the Capitol (a magnificent temple where heroes are honoured) and the Senate-house close by, where the Senate itself is to be imagined as assembled to honour Caesar on his triumphant return. There has also to be some representation of a statue of Pompey, in accordance with lines 119–20: Caesar, stabbed to death, not only lies obscurely, 'No worthier than the dust', but at the feet of Pompey, who the crowd had once praised to the skies, and then dropped from their esteem and replaced with their latest hero, Caesar. (This was all more than

Marullus could bear, at I.i.31ff.) Despite such considerations, however, do you think the place where he lies should be given at least a certain amount of prominence, even though nothing in the nature of a platform or dais? You will not require a 'pulpit' for the funeral orations until the next scene, but it is significant that a 'pulpit' is mentioned twice in this scene (82, 86), anticipating the scene in the Forum when the body is brought in from the market-place, and therefore calling for some emphasis.

As you see, the set has to be a complicated one. You will need to prepare a plan for it which despite its complexity leaves easy passages for the crowd in the street, and easy access for the characters who come and go (Antony, Trebonius, Antony's servant, Octavius's Servant).

Lighting

By the time this scene is reached in the play, the storm is over and the sun is fully up. There seems to us no reason why the lighting at any point should be dimmed, e.g. to point up the horror of the assassination. On the contrary, we think there is much to be said for all the action in this scene taking place in the full glare of the Mediterranean sunshine. But you may think differently, especially if you decide that, despite what we have already said about costume, you are going to use spotlights to draw attention to key speakers and centres of action.

Movement on the stage ('Blocking')

The bigger the crowd of characters to appear together on the stage, the more carefully their movement and their reactions to one another have to be planned. Enough has been said already in these notes to emphasise how complex such movement and interaction are going to be in this scene; a minute-by-minute plan needs to be prepared, so as to ensure that nothing remains static in this fast-moving sequence of events.

Here are two examples of points of interaction and coordination which need to be thought out carefully, with your stage-set in your mind, before you come to required decisions.

First is the whole matter of the petitions to Caesar leading up to his assassination, from virtually the beginning of the scene up to the stabbing: Are you going to take these entirely at their face value? Are the petitions genuine and spontaneous? Or, except for Artemidorus's, are they all contrived and coordinated so as to engage Caesar in this sort of state business, and in this way surround him with conspirators! Your answers to these questions will guide you as to how to direct the movements of the characters implicated here, especially Popilius's, since the doubt about his role in the plot is not fully resolved; and also the formality or otherwise of the way people move up to Caesar, as in the case of Metellus Cimber (27).

Second, the doubts about Antony must surely be communicated very clearly, even though he is not always on the stage to do this himself. His exit at 26 indicates that the assured conspirators have suspicions of his devotion to the cause; they have arranged for Trebonius to get Antony 'out of the way'. But, unlike Trebonius, Antony does not come back at 99, and is reported as having gone home in amazement at what has happened. However, he must not be lost sight of, because these events are the prelude to his rise to power. It is his servant who comes seeking assurances (genuinely, do you think?) and again his re-entry is prepared for. After his exchange with Brutus and Cassius and the granting of his wish to speak at the funeral, he is left alone for his great speech beginning, 'O pardon me, thou bleeding piece of earth' (258 ff) and finishes the scene with only Octavius's servant by his side, another strong portent of the new order. You will need to work out how, despite distractions, this sequencing of events and ideas remains intact.

Speech

You will undoubtedly find that your actors enjoy speaking the lines. They are full of Shakespeare's magic, the magic that makes them sound very like normal, everyday speech yet preserves the rhythmic swell of the verse-line (see p. ix). They are as appropriate for soft, thoughtful addresses to single hearers (e.g. 'O mighty Caesar! . . . 152–4) as for loud declamations of firmly-held beliefs ('I know not, gentlemen' . . . 155–167), and the alteration of tone, even within a single speech (as in the lines referred to just now) has to be carefully contrasted.

Here are some points where you will need to direct your actors in the amount of emphasis, if any, they are to give to what they are saying:

– 'ordinary' (38) – Caesar is contrasting himself with ordinary men;

– 'What, Brutus!' (56) – is this Caesar's premonition of his cry *'Et tu Brute'* as he dies (79)?

– lines 218–9 – the exchange between Brutus and Antony (183–213, ending with Antony's moving imagery of the hart) is about both love for Caesar and the rightness of the plot to kill him; but Cassius is evidently impatient to find out whose side Antony is on; hence the most effective scanning of these lines seems to be:

I bláme you nót for práising Cáesar só,

But whát compáct mean yóu to háve with *ús*?

i.e. 'Caesar' contrasting with 'us' by means of extra emphasis.

– 'O Caesar!' (285) – how is this to indicate, by intonation as well as stress, that the Servant first notices Caesar's body at this moment, and is astounded by what he sees?

Sound effects

If you do not have a large crowd of extras, some effects of the noise of an excited crowd may be needed to reinforce that of the actors in the named parts. Would you agree that no other special sound effects are required? Certainly there is no need for a trumpet, say, to herald the arrival of Caesar, because he is here concerned to mix with the ordinary people as well as his noble companions, and to take petitions from anyone. Similarly at the end of the scene a solemn march in music would be quite inappropriate, since his body is carried off, not in procession but by just two people, one of them a servant.

To sum up, the points made here and the questions posed could be extended indefinitely, because the scene is so rich in word and action. When you come to write your answer, however, you will need to limit it by arranging your points under a set of headings such as those suggested above, and in this way set out a plan for your production. A plan built up in this way, written out clearly and briefly and supported by sketches, could be the account which the examiners are asking for.